Willie Pep vs. Sandy Saddler

Notes on the Boxing Legends and Epic Rivalry

Doug Werner

Tracks Publishing
San Diego, California

Willie Pep vs. Sandy Saddler
Notes on the Boxing Legends and Epic Rivalry
Doug Werner

Tracks Publishing
140 Brightwood Avenue
Chula Vista, CA 91910
619-476-7125
tracks@cox.net
www.startupsports.com
trackspublishing.com

Copyright © 2014 by Doug Werner
10 9 8 7 6 5 4 3 2 1

Publisher's Cataloging-in-Publication

Werner, Doug, 1950-

Willie Pep vs. Sandy Saddler : notes on the boxing legends and epic rivalry / Doug Werner. -- San Diego, California : Tracks Publishing, c2014.

p. ; cm.

ISBN: 978-1-935937-57-9
Includes bibliographical references and index.
Summary: Any discussion of great boxers must include Willie Pep and Sandy Saddler, midcentury featherweight champions whose heroics in the 1940s and 1950s electrified the fistic world then and reverberate today. This book explores the boxing lives of both pugilists' early years, fighting years, training and conditioning, historical context, life after boxing, and of course, the lasting controversy over their rivalry and legacy. Their matchups had it all: contrasting styles, dazzling skills, hard punching, splendid action, ridiculous brawling, heroic victories and crashing defeats.--Publisher.

1. Pep, Willie. 2. Saddler, Sandy. 3. Boxers (Sports)--Biography. 4. Boxing--United States--History. 5. Boxers (Sports)--Training--History. 6. Boxing matches--United States--History.

GV1131 .W47 2014   2014936461
796.8/30922--dc23   1407

To
Kathleen and Joy
You have given me everything

Special thanks
to
Phyllis Carter
Editor extraordinaire

Contents

Photo credits for this book
Bettman/Corbis
Cover, back cover, photo insert after page 114

Library of Congress
Pages 16, 19, 20, 23, 24, 25, 29, 30, 38, 39, 43, 47, 51, 52, 55, 71, 82, 103

Willie Pep vs. Sandy Saddler

Not in 100 years

[They] fought each other in four celebrated bouts, including (so they say) the best fight in boxing history and the worst.

Who <u>are</u> these guys?

For our last publication, *Boxer's Bible of Counterpunching*, author Mark Hatmaker made a list of great counter artists. The name at the top was Willie Pep. I wondered who that was. Although I had a fair knowledge of great middleweight and heavyweight boxers, apparently this guy Pep was the best boxer I never heard of. So I looked him up. Boy, what a fighter — over 200 wins! And what a character — six wives!

Then I read about the four epic battles he waged with Sandy Saddler and how he lost three of them. The clash of styles yielded some of the best boxing ever witnessed ... and some of the worst. *How could that be?* And who was this guy Saddler? I discovered that he was something of a physical oddity, an unlikely power puncher who knocked out 103 of the fighters he faced. And although he ripped Pep, he was, and is, usually considered a lesser boxer among boxing historians and prominent list makers. *Why is that?*

At any rate, my initial interest in the great boxing career of Pep grew to include Saddler until the writing project became (quite naturally) a study of both.

Pep was the epitome of the boxing maxim — make them miss and make them pay.

At first I was prepared to like Pep over Saddler because I bought into the pure boxer vs. dirty fighter thing. The blazing artist, victorious in so many fights (who survived a plane crash, for heaven's sake) vs. the plodding slugger, who won by thuggery and, well, just didn't look like anybody's boxing hero.

Then I got to work and began to learn more about both guys. I started to think that maybe Saddler got a raw deal. He wasn't a beautiful fighter, sure. But he won. He destroyed opponents. He destroyed Pep, but it seems (sometimes) like that's overlooked or explained away somehow in Pep's favor. He was rough all right, but so was Pep. Just look at the photos and the film. I also started to like this quieter man who didn't smoke, drink or curse. When he won his first title, he brought home a bag of cookies and soda pop to share with his brothers and sisters to help him celebrate (he still lived with his parents at the time). Does that sound like a mean, nasty fellow?

And now? Well, maybe I'm equally enamored. How can you choose one over the other? Both fought their hearts out. Both were great winners. In 100 years there will not be another Pep who won so many fights or another Saddler who knocked out more than five score men. Did one guy wear the belt better than the other? Pep was outgoing and Saddler was not. Pep was funny and charming. Saddler knew how to smile, but he wasn't glib. Sometimes he wouldn't even answer a reporter's question (actually, I find that endearing).

Brilliant performer

Willie Pep stood five foot, five and a half inches and had a reach of 68 inches — fairly long arms for a short man. Outside of that, he owned a conventional frame for a featherweight boxer ... or a professional dancer.

The outstanding characteristic of his presence in the ring was movement. His head and shoulders moved up and down to control the vertical plane of action. His legs moved him forward, backward and side to side in an endless effort to create angles and to control the vertical plane. He avoided the incoming punches and countered into all the holes his opponent left unattended. Pep was the epitome of the boxing maxim — make them miss and make them pay. His way was brilliant performance — athletic, even artistic, and loads of fun to watch.

Gaunt destroyer

Sandy Saddler was five foot, eight and a half inches tall. About average height for a man in America at the time, but certainly not for a featherweight boxer weighing in at 126 pounds max. He was always tall in the ring, sometimes towering over guys who stood a bit over 60 inches. He had very long arms. His reach was 70 inches — two inches longer than heavyweight icon Rocky Marciano! When you first saw Saddler in the ring, you were struck by his tall, skinny frame. *Can this guy really hit? Can he take a punch?*

Then you noticed the naked aggression — a ceaseless effort to get his man. He knew how to move his feet and fold himself up to ward off blows. He certainly knew how to jab at range and then to unfold and use hooks and uppercuts in close to devastating effect.

Oh, he knew what he was doing in there. Maybe every bit as much as Pep. But he was never pretty to look at. Saddler was gaunt, all arms and legs. His frenzied attack struck some as "ludicrous" — especially when "drooling froth from his gaping mouth."[1]

Everybody loved this winner

His ring name fit the fighter — Pep was actually quite the peppy fellow. He was also quick with a smile and always had something amusing to say. He was proud, but with a twinkle in his eye and a dash of modesty. The combination of liveliness, good cheer and humility was infectious. And, of course, he was a winner. Pep was a very popular man his entire life.

A hard man

Saddler was reserved and straightforward. He eschewed the usual vices. He was described as a "hard man" who "liked to do things his way."[2] As a man of few words, he never ingratiated himself to the press. His taciturnity was so pronounced that in reading his quotes today one can hardly help but laugh. But at the time many were put off. He appeared sullen, perhaps a bit menacing with little to counter the bad boy stuff.

Other than his winning ways, he wasn't an appealing public figure. He was a "rough" fighter, no stranger to illegal boxing, who just didn't look like any boxer

Then you noticed the naked aggression — a ceaseless effort to get his man.

anyone had ever seen in the ring before. His fighting acumen was overshadowed by his height and reach advantages — fans thought matchups with shorter men were unfair. He was booed at times and even instigated a riot or two. His victories over Pep were grudgingly accepted at best. Saddler was an unpopular champion compared to his archrival, and this painted his career and life until the end.

Crazy fast

Pep was a natural. He was crazy fast with his hands and feet and knew pretty much right away the key to his success would be hitting the other guy more than the other guy hit him. He learned that on the streets dodging the big boys who wanted to push him around. Pep could punch some, of course — he KO'd 65 and broke at least one jaw over the run of his career — but his bread and butter was pure boxing and always would be. It was when he deviated from the stick and move that he suffered his few ring failures.

All he needed was someone who could fine tune his whirling dervish. That guy was trainer Bill Gore. He took one look at Pep, closed shop in Miami and went north to Hartford to forge his masterpiece along with manager Lou Viscusi who took care of the business and marketing of the golden boy.

The smartest thing Pep ever did as a fighter was to stick

Like Pep, Saddler listened to his trainers, became an A student and was intelligent enough to stick with these gents throughout his fistic journey.

with these guys and listen to everything Gore had to say. He took it all in — learned how to fight behind a busy jab and move — in and out, side-to-side, from every angle. Just as important as the boxing skills he taught, Gore brought a presence that suited the combustible Pep to a T. Gore was a steady sage and calm counterpoint to the ever jumpy Pep.

Get him! Get him! Get him!

Saddler was born with punching power and a killer instinct. Instead of Pep's catch-me-if-you-can, Saddler was the ultimate presser. Or as George Foreman would say about his former trainer, it was always "Get him, get him, get him!"[3] Saddler was a knockout artist from the get-go, scoring a remarkable 103 KOs in his fighting life. Saddler was discovered early on by manager Charlie Johnston who guided the young slugger throughout his career and provided perhaps the greatest coach/trainer/mentor a young boxer could ever have in one Archie Moore.

Moore was a fighter in Johnston's stable and a great champion in his own right, but he took a shine to the younger Saddler and taught him how to box and punch even harder. (Moore is the all-time knockout artist with 131 KOs.) Saddler had an official trainer in Bertie

Constant conditioning

Conditioning for fighters of this era was an ongoing process and unless interrupted by accident, illness or injury, quite constant. Fights were fought once or twice every month. There was hardly time to fall off the wagon.

Training always included roadwork (or running) to build/maintain endurance, bag work, core work with medicine balls and sparring. The latter was always specific to the opponent. Partners were chosen who could fight like the guy they'd have to box next. News articles that came out before each fight often listed sparring partners and tallied the number of sparring rounds each fighter had accumulated.

What was not part of the program was serious weight lifting. There may have been a bit with smaller weights, but boxers did not bulk up for fear of losing speed and reaction time. It was felt that necessary muscle development and strength for boxing was best obtained through a normal training routine. Punching effectiveness and especially power was thought to be a function of "balance, leverage, coordination, speed and timing."[4] Bunched up muscles got in the way of that. Boxers boxed to get in shape. They did not pump iron.

Briscoe (and should not be short changed), but one of Briscoe's finer attributes was what he did *not* do — he never interfered with the learning arrangements between Moore and Saddler.

Like Pep, Saddler listened to his trainers, became an A student and was intelligent enough to stick with these gents throughout his fistic journey. By temperament, Saddler was self-contained. Easy going and amiable outside the ring, he took a laser focus into battle and never needed encouragement to charge into his foe.

Lucky and wise

Both fighters were extremely lucky to end up with suitable trainers, and most wise to listen and stay with them. Coupled with their natural abilities and passion for the game, they grew into two of the finest fighters in boxing history.

In the end, this book is a recognition of two boxing giants. A respectful story of two boys who became very great fighters, who fought each other in four celebrated bouts, including (so they say) the best fight in boxing history and the worst. If nothing else, I hope my modest effort shines a light on these two men so people will know and remember because they most certainly deserve it.

Sources for Not in 100 years

espn.com

New York Post

Pittsburgh Post-Gazette

Silver, Mike. *The Arc of Boxing*. Jefferson, North Carolina: McFarland & Company, Inc., 2008.

Footnotes for Not in 100 years

1 Jimmy Cannon, "Willie Pep Turns Quitter," *New York Post*, February 14, 1999.
2 *Pittsburgh Post-Gazette*, September 21, 2001, from Tim Smith, "Sandy Saddler, Former Boxing Champion," *New York Daily News*.
3 George Foreman, *Saddler was vicious in ring*, October 11, 2001, http://sports.espn.go.com/espn/classic/news/story?page=foreman_on_saddler
4 Mike Silver, *The Arc of Boxing* (Jefferson: McFarland & Company, Inc., 2008), 180.

"I can lick any son of a bitch in the house!" — John L. Sullivan, boxing's first superstar.

1. Historical overview

Bare-knuckle boxing was a mix of punching, grappling (from the waist up) and throwing.

Bare-knuckle beginnings

Fencing begat bare-knuckle boxing in 18th century England. It was thought that the finality of a fencing bout was too final. One could fight another day (albeit often following a long, long rest) after a boxing match.

Bare-knuckle boxing was a mix of punching, grappling (from the waist up) and throwing. A round ended when one of the fighters hit the turf. Matches were held outside in a roped-off area to keep the howling throngs at bay. Seconds or assistants helped the fallen man back to his corner for a 30-second rest, and he had another eight seconds to toe the mark (on his own) in the center of the ring. If he could not come to scratch, he was considered knocked out and lost. A bare-knuckle bout was a fight to the finish by said KO or disqualification via fouling. Fouls included kicking, gouging, striking a man when down, head butting and biting.

Queensberry Rules

By the mid-1800s a new set of boxing rules were introduced that greatly refined the sport. The Marquis of Queensberry Rules disallowed throwing and wrestling, established the three-minute round with a minute

The most important change by far was the requirement of padded gloves.

respite between each round, and the 10-second count after a knockdown.

The most important change by far was the requirement of padded gloves. Gloves protected the hands and allowed fighters to strike temple and jaw with a force and frequency that would have broken unprotected fingers before. Unhesitant boxers unleashed powerful, crowd-pleasing punches.

Fights moved indoors and boxers performed on a raised platform. Fighters tossed the spikes and wore leather-soled shoes that led to swifter and more mobile foot-work. Promoters began to charge admission. The new arrangement allowed for greater crowd control and a safer, more genteel environment suitable for a wider audience.

Science

The end of the bare-knuckle era is usually associated with the first heavyweight championship fight con-ducted under Queensberry Rules in 1892 when Gentleman Jim Corbett defeated Boston Strong Boy John L. Sullivan in New Orleans. The bout is also significant because the "Boxer" beat the "Slugger" (although Corbett could indeed punch, knocking out Sullivan in the 21st round). Wearing five-ounce gloves, Corbett used foot-work, counterpunching and a constant left jab to con-fuse and conquer the powerful champion.

What Gentleman Jim did that evening so many years ago

JAMES J. CORBETT.

is what so many great boxers have done since in similar circumstances. As Mike Silver says in his wonderful book, *The Arc of Boxing*, Corbett used, "the effective application of the art of boxing to defeat an opponent possessing superior strength and power..."[1]

Corbett influenced other fighters to use the brainier, more tactical approach. His refined technique (relative to the age) is the reason he is remembered as the father of scientific boxing.

Breaking the color barrier in the 19th century

The Corbett vs. Sullivan match was held over a three-day period called the *Carnival of Champions* and also featured featherweight champion George Dixon, who happened to be the first-ever black titlist. This is significant (and a little amazing) because he was, indeed, a black champion who fought caucasians (openly) before the turn of the century.

It certainly can be argued that boxing, in it's own stumbling way, led the sports world in this regard. Boxing was rife with racism as the new century unfolded, but increasing numbers of blacks built substantial careers with their fists. This is especially noteworthy if compared with African-American acceptance in other sports

The brilliant George Dixon may have fought 800 times.

(or most any other endeavor with a degree of status). For example, Jackie Robinson didn't break the color barrier in major league baseball until he signed with the Brooklyn Dodgers in 1946.

Wild West

Until the 1920s, public prizefighting was illegal in most states. Matches had to be held in secret locations or as so-called "sparring sessions" in private clubs. Boxers were sometimes jailed and some fights fixed. Events could be dangerous to spectators due to police raids or eruptions of violence.

Because states in the western United States had fewer restrictions, activity there dominated boxing in the early 20th century. From 1910 to 1919, 60 title fights were held in California (compared to 10 in New York and six in England). The west also saw the rise of promoters James Coffroth and Tex Rickard — the latter arguably promoting the biggest and most influential boxing extravaganzas ever.

The former Rough Rider was in truth a boxing advocate having boxed at Harvard and encouraged law enforcement and the YMCA to include it in their fitness programs.

New York and boxing from 1900 to 1920

A bewildering slew of New York state laws were of considerable influence from around 1900 to 1920 (New York, especially New York City, being the center of the universe). New York had criminalized most aspects of prizefighting in 1859. Not that it stopped the boys from mixing it up — bouts went underground.

The Horton Law sort of legalized boxing from 1896-1900. Prizefighting was still out, but "... sparring exhibitions with gloves of not less than five ounces each in weight may be held by a domestic incorporated athletic association in a building leased by it for athletic purposes only for at least one year, or in a building owned and occupied by such association." NY Laws, 1896, Ch. 301, Sec. 458.

The Horton Law was repealed by the Lewis Law and officially expired in 1900. Then Governor Teddy Roosevelt endorsed this, and it should be noted that it was because of the corrupting influence of gambling — specifically fight fixing — that motivated him. The former Rough Rider was in truth a boxing advocate having boxed at Harvard and encouraged law enforcement and the

With the Walker Law, the center of boxing activity shifted to New York. Boxing became a legitimate athletic pursuit and drove to new heights of popularity.

YMCA to include it in their fitness programs. TR kept it up later in life until a thumb detached a retina. After that he wrestled in the White House and took all comers.

The Frawley Act permitted professional boxing from 1911 to 1917 until a fighter, Young McDonald, was killed in the ring. Boxing was then prohibited in the state until the 1920 Walker Law. The Frawley Act is remembered mostly for its insistence on no-decision fight results. That is, if no fighter was knocked out after the final bell, the match was rendered a no-decision — no winner, no loser. It was thought that if only a KO could decide a match, the chance for illicit influence would be curtailed. But as things worked out, newspaper reporters took it upon themselves to pick a winner, gamblers took their cue, and in a number of ways, this proved a wobbly way to do things and thus corrupted the game.

The Walker Law legalized professional boxing in New York State, established a number of regulations including standard weight divisions and called for an agency to oversee the sport. This was to be the New York State Athletic Commission (NYSAC). It is said that the Walker

TR threw leather.

Law was heavily influenced by the rules and weights established for the American Expeditionary Force (AEF) Boxing Tournament of 1919 in England.

The Walker Law stood and influenced several states to adopt similar programs. With the Walker Law, the center of boxing activity shifted to New York. Boxing became a legitimate athletic pursuit and drove to new heights of popularity. There came the million dollar gates and the larger than life heroics of Jack Dempsey and Gene Tunney. Of course, this is of a piece with the "Golden Age of Sport" — the 1920s — that produced baseball's Babe Ruth and Lou Gehrig; Tennis's Bill Tilden; footballs's Red Grange; Golf's Bobby Jones and Walter Hagen.

The first main event conducted under this new law was the Joe Welling vs. Johnny Dundee bout. (Dundee, the "Scotch Wop," is a featured featherweight in the next chapter.)

Classic eight
The first decade of the 20th century began with six weight classes and ended up with eight (much to the relief of the smaller boxer).

Flyweight (112 lbs.)
Bantamweight (118 lbs.)

Featherweight (126 lbs.)
Lightweight (135 lbs.)
Welterweight (147 lbs.)
Middleweight (160 lbs.)
Light Heavyweight (175 lbs.)
Heavyweight (unlimited)

Modern boxing

By the second decade of the century the majority of bouts were limited to 10 rounds or less — and boxing went uptempo. Characteristics of the new era fighting included mobile footwork, counterpunching, effective use of power and defensive skills such as slipping, parrying and blocking. The public loved the science and lapped it up — fighters and their fights were brought to a wider audience via film, radio and newspapers.

Dempsey

During WWI, boxing was used to entertain and condition troops headed for duty in Europe. *The Ring* magazine, established in 1922, became the advocate, arbitrator and beacon for boxing and remains so to this day.

Tex Rickard, Jack Dempsey and the Golden Age

Times were ripe for a riproaring promoter like Tex Rickard. This guy was a singular character — he operated a gambling house in the Alaskan Klondike during the 1890s gold rush, punched cows in Texas and even sheriffed for a spell. Like Buffalo Bill Cody, he brought some of the Wild West into the American mainstream, albeit roughneck boxers instead of thundering calvary.

U.S. MARINES

Who needs guns?

"Supermen with their fists"

According to an article[2] in the first issue of *The Ring* (February 1922), boxing was "rejuvenated" by World War One. Before that time boxing "was classed as brutal, as debasing, followed only by the rough, the uncultured, the vicious." But fisticuffs played a major role in the "Great War," especially for our very green troops. The United States entered the conflict unprepared. Our soldiers were "unschooled in the military arts, unfitted by temperament, by character, for fostering brutal warfare." But they had "one sublime attribute ... an almost common knowledge of the manly art of self-defense." Seeing this, U.S. military authorities decided to base the training of recruits in boxing. "It proved to be the greatest foundation a military machine could have had."

From this credible assertion the article goes further to argue that boxing was much more than a training tool. It inspired extreme courage in the face of a wicked, powerful enemy. Fists could overwhelm guns and bullets!

"[Boxing] was baptized in blood at the Marne when the Marines charged, came to grips and, throwing aside the cumbersome rifle ... struck out with their fists and never ... failed to drop the target."

This is a reference to the Battle of Belleau Wood fought in June, 1918. In this pivotal battle, United States Marines "beat back five German counterattacks, fighting off more than four divisions of crack German troops. They did it with their rifles, their bayonets and sometimes with their fists."[3]

According to *The Ring*, this and other similar incidents uplifted the art of boxing, even glorified it. The article says, "No wonder that after that the world looked upon our 'leather-necks' and 'doughboys' as supermen, for supermen they were, and are. It is in their blood. It is part of their natural existence to be boxers, supermen with their fists."

Almost overnight Rickard "transformed professional boxing into popular entertainment for a mass audience."

He promoted the Joe Gans vs. Battling Nelson lightweight title fight in Goldfield, Nevada in 1906. In 1910 he promoted the first of his "Fights of the Century" between heavyweights Jim Jeffries and Jack Johnson. Then he came east and sparked the aforementioned "Golden Age of Sport."

On July 4, 1921, he promoted the Jack Dempsey vs. Georges Carpentier title fight in New Jersey (just across the Hudson River from New York City). The crowd of 90,000 was the largest ever for a sporting event up to that time and was the first million-dollar gate. Dempsey earned $300,000 for 12 minutes of work (it took him four rounds to demolish Carpentier). And this was the first time a championship bout was broadcast on radio. The July 5, 1921 *The New York Times* featured the fight in all eight columns on the front page. Almost overnight Rickard "transformed professional boxing into popular entertainment for a mass audience."[4]

Boxing arrives

The money generated by these boxing events did not go unnoticed by other states. The tax revenues became a glittering prize. The anti-boxing forces were trampled. In 1917, 23 states allowed professional boxing. By 1925 there were 43. Boxing became a growth industry and, in the first half of the 20th century, it would rival baseball as America's most popular spectator sport. Stars of the ring were the highest paid athletes in the world. A popular boxer could earn $10,000 per bout. An average professional baseball player made $8,000 a year. Babe Ruth made $80,000 each season. Gene Tunney made a million for his second fight with Dempsey.

And there was a bit of trickling down from the upper reaches. Silver says, "A lowly bucket carrier could earn a modest living working corners up to six nights a week."[6]

In cities across America, countless young men took up boxing. Arenas popped up. Inner city gyms were filled with aspiring fighters. New York City became the center of the boxing universe. In the 1920s, more than two dozen arenas operated on a weekly or bimonthly basis within 10 miles of Times Square.

Boxing cartoons in the New Yorker [5]

How do you gauge the success of something? Here's an eye-opener if you read one of America's venerable (and more highbrow) magazines, the *New Yorker*. Famous for its cartoons, boxing was featured in a great many of them in the early to mid-20th century — not so much these days.

1930-1949	57
1950-1969	55
1970-1989	9
1990-2009	4

In 1925 the NYSAC annual report stated that 1,890 licensed pro fighters resided in the state, up from 1,654 the year before. In 1927 the number was 2,000 with over 900 boxing shows throughout the state. During the 1920s and 1930s, 8,000 to 10,000 pro boxers were licensed annually in the United States.

For boys growing up in the 1930s, boxing was a popular and organized pursuit. Little League Baseball didn't exist.

Into mainstream America, boxing in the 1920s

Boxing was mainstream and had been so since the dramatic rise of heavyweights Jack Dempsey, Gene Tunney and the million dollar gates of the 1920s. Some 120,000 people saw their first fight in Philadelphia in 1926 and more than 104,000 witnessed the second in Chicago in 1927.

Besides these legends, the decade was full of more Hall of Famers. Benny Leonard, lightweight champion, was known for his speed, technical ability and intelligence. Harry Grebe won middleweight and light heavyweight belts and was the only boxer to defeat Gene Tunney. He fought his last 90 fights blind in one eye. Tiger Flowers became the first African American middleweight champion. Mickey Walker won middleweight and welterweight titles. Tommy Loughran was a light heavyweight champion known for his footwork, defensive skills and counterpunching.

Boxing in the 1930s

The Great Depression of the 1930s dampened the numbers, but enthusiasm for boxing was mighty. After all, these years saw the rise of Joe Louis. As these things go, heavyweight events led the way: Jack Sharkey and Max Schmeling drew 61,863 in 1932. Max Baer and James

Barney Ross was a great champion and war hero.

Braddock scrapped in front of 35,000 in 1934. Joe Louis and Braddock attracted 45,500 in 1937. Eighty thousand delirious fans watched Joe Louis defeat Max Schmeling at Yankee Stadium in 1938, and *The New York Times* made that battle front page news the next day. Of course, millions of fans worldwide listened to these events on their radios.

It would be a mistake to ignore the careers of some of the lighter class fighters. Tony Canzoneri and Barney Ross each won titles in three divisions or weight classes. Canzoneri, an Italian American hero, won the featherweight, lightweight and light welterweight titles.

Ross, a hugely influential and popular Jewish American, won the lightweight, light welterweight and welterweight titles. At a time when the Jew was especially denigrated here and abroad, his fighting career shattered stereotypes and inspired a generation to stand tall.

Boxing for boys in the 1930s

Willie Pep was born in 1922. He was 10 years old in 1932. Sandy Saddler was born in 1926 and would be 10 years old in 1936. What was the state of sports in America like back then?

For boys growing up in the 1930s, boxing was a popular and organized pursuit. Little League Baseball didn't exist.

Joe Louis (left) was every boy's hero in the '30s.

Pop Warner Football was only beginning. There was zero soccer. No skateboarding, snowboarding or surfing. No video games! Pep's Connecticut (and New England) and Saddler's New York City were especially rife with boxing activity. Boys were encouraged to learn the manly art at venues such as the YMCA, Young Mens Hebrew Association (YMHA), Police Athletic League (PAL), Catholic Youth Association (CYA) and various other clubs and gyms. In 1923, the *Chicago Tribune* sponsored the first Golden Gloves Tournament and challenged boxers from New York City. Soon it would grow into a much respected national organization. There was boxing across the land in high schools and colleges.

Glory days and heros to emulate

Boxing was on the upswing and its unseemly, unsafe reputation was in the past (or at least varnished for the time being) and in the future. In the 1930s, champions like Barney Ross, Tony Canzoneri, Henry Armstrong and especially Joe Louis were highly regarded and considered worthy role models.

Why they got serious about boxing

First generation kids of immigrant parents saw boxing prowess as a means to gain status in the city neighborhoods and a way to make a buck during hard times. For a select few, among them Willie Pep and Sandy Saddler, it meant fame and fortune or at least a fair shot at success in a depressed world with few options.

Sources for Chapter 1

boxrec.com

Clement, Priscilla Ferguson and Reinier, Jacqueline S. *Boyhood in America: An Encylcopedia*. Santa Barbara, California: ABC-CLIO, Inc., 2001.

cyberboxing.com

eastsideboxing.com

Manhoff, Robert. *Boxing Days*, http://www.newyorker.com/online/blogs/cartoonists/2011/11/boxing-days.html#ixzz2HW13bszq (November 9, 2011).

Roberts, James B. and Skutt, Alexander G. *The Boxing Register*. Ithaca, New York: McBooks Press, Inc., 2011.

Silver, Mike. *The Arc of Boxing*. Jefferson, North Carolina: McFarland & Company, Inc., 2008.

The Ring. *1920s: Article from the first issue of THE RING*, http://ringtv.craveonline.com/blog/170425-1920s (December 1, 2011).

Weston, Stanley and Farhood, Steven. *The Ring: Boxing The 20th Century*. New York: BDD Illustrated Books, 1993.

Footnotes Chapter 1

1 Mike Silver, *The Arc of Boxing* (Jefferson: McFarland & Company, Inc., 2008), 7.
2 The Ring, *1920s: Article from the first issue of THE RING*, http://ringtv.craveonline.com/blog/170425-1920s (December 1, 2011).
3 Linda D. Kozaryn, *Marines' First Crucible: Belleau Wood*, http://www.defense.gov/News/NewsArticle.aspx?ID=43169 (June 6, 1998).
4 Mike Silver, *The Arc of Boxing* (Jefferson: McFarland & Company, Inc., 2008), 24-25.
5 Robert Manhoff, *Boxing Days*, http://www.newyorker.com/online/blogs/cartoonists/2011/11/boxing-days.html#ixzz2HW13bszq (November 9, 2011).
6 Mike Silver, *The Arc of Boxing* (Jefferson: McFarland & Company, Inc., 2008), 26.

Willie Pep vs. Sandy Saddler

Photos
Images in this section and the next from the Library of Congress.

2. Fine feathers

Although the two fighters brought their own unique personalities and boxing styles into the ring, there certainly were a passel of commonalities with their feather forebears.

Finest feathers from 1900 to 1942
From the turn of the last century until the reigns of Willie Pep and Sandy Saddler, there were a number of great feathers. Included in the next few pages are some of the best. They were chosen for a variety of reasons. All won at least a featherweight title, a few won titles in other weight classes as well. Most held on to their belt or belts for more than a few weeks or months. All are ranked highly by boxing historians and over time have maintained or gained stature. So they were great boxers.

This overview also provides foundation for understanding the fighting and the fighting world of Pep and Saddler. Although the two fighters brought their own unique personalities and boxing styles into the ring, there certainly were a passel of commonalities with their feather forebears. And it can be shown that there was a bit of foreshadowing of things to come before their time.

Henry Armstrong lost fights he should have won because he was half starved.

Immigrants

The group includes a cross section of America or, to be more precise, New Americans during the first 40 years or so of the 20th century. Most were sons of immigrants. A couple were fresh off the boat. Those who were not citizens and chose not to stay were American enough in their ambitions. They each saw boxing as a way to get ahead.

From everywhere

They were a diverse bunch — Irish, Jewish, Sicilian, Welsh, West Indian, French ...

Henry Armstrong was African American, Native American and Irish all by himself.

Kid Chocolate was Cuban (certainly a descendant of African slaves), and for a heady time about as American or Americanized as a temporary transplant could be.

Jim Driscoll was Welsh (cauliflower ears and all).

Eugene Crique was French.

Some say Chalky Wright's grandfather was a runaway slave and his immediate family cowboys.

Sandy Saddler's father was a transplant from the Carribean.

Hardscrabble

Most had hardscrabble stories. Most were shooting stars.

Imagine in the same life to be so poor you stay hungry for days, but then fortune strikes and you sit at a table with some of the most famous people on earth. Henry Armstrong lost fights he should have won because he was half starved. But then came a time he would drink and dine with the likes of Al Jolson, George Raft and Mae West — Hollywood royalty.

They all came from humble beginnings:

Chalky Wright never knew his father.

Kid Chocolate was a street urchin.

Johnny Dundee worked at a fish market in Hell's Kitchen, no less.

Battling Battalino toiled in tobacco fields.

Willie Pep's father made 15 dollars a week working for the WPA. Pep helped out by shinning shoes.

True grit

All of these men were very, very tough.

Eugene Criqui had his jaw shot off in the first world war and had it put together with animal bone and wire. With that jaw and a champion's fortitude, he KO'd Johnny Kilbane for the title.

Battling Battalino defeated Andre Routis for the featherweight title with two broken hands.

Jim Driscoll worked a tent at carnivals where he took on scores of challengers each day.

Frequent fighters
These men fought many, many fights.

Eight had at least 100 total bouts. Seven had more than 150. Freddie Miller had 252 fights totaling 2,028 rounds. Johnny Dundee had 341 bouts in 21 years — over 3,000 rounds of boxing.

Betting and thrown fights
Gambling is sports greatest enemy. Its influence attracts criminals, subverts athletic achievement and destroys lives. Boxing has struggled with it from day one. More than other sports? It's tempting to say yes and with some reason, but that would be unfair in the end. No sport is pure or safe from those looking for an advantage.

But boxing, perhaps like no other, has the gaudy reputation replete with mobsters, showmen and broken fighters that has always made for great stories. There is a romance to it in this game that doesn't take in, say, baseball or basketball where fixing is truly shameful and repercussions harsh.

These feathers were touched by betting:

Terry McGovern faced Joe Gans in 1900. Gans took a dive in the second round.

Abe Attell openly bet on himself and associated with

Johnny Dundee had 341 bouts in 21 years — over 3,000 rounds of boxing.

Arnold Rothstein. He allegedly took part in one of the darkest scandals in American sport history — the fix of the 1919 World Series.

In January 1932, Battling Battalino faced Freddie Miller. The referee eventually stopped the bout because Battalino showed little enthusiasm for the contest. Bat was stripped of the featherweight belt, and Miller lost his standing as a contender (he was dropped from *The Ring* magazine's annual rankings).

In March 1940, Henry Armstrong fought middleweight champ Ceferino Garcia to a draw. It is said that he was offered $75,000 to take a dive, but refused. At least one historian, Bert Sugar, says Armstrong won the title bout with Garcia, but that the draw was "prearranged."

Chalky Wright gambled his ring earnings away (an old story, that), took menial work, lost his wife and moved in with his mother. She found him dead in the bathtub.

Willie Pep sued *Newsweek, Inc.* over an article that said he had thrown a fight. He lost the court battle and claimed the damage to his reputation cost him a commissioner's job.

In the arena
Each man has a story and a tale of glory.

Some were hard hitters who inspired fear, and some

were artful boxers who befuddled their foes.

Some went on to enjoy a life away from boxing and many did not.

Some were scoundrels and some straight arrows.

Some loud and brash, others quiet and thoughtful.

Some soared high and bright and some burned out.

They all loved to fight.

Each one stepped into the ring with courage and fortitude and should be honored and remembered for that.

Another great warrior said it best:

IT IS NOT THE CRITIC who counts; not the man who points out how the strong man stumbles, or where the doer of deeds could have done them better. The credit belongs to the man who is actually in the arena, whose face is marred by dust and sweat and blood; who strives valiantly ...

—Theodore Roosevelt

Terry McGovern
Terrible Terry
60-5-4, 44 KOs
80 total bouts

Terrible Terry McGovern's style was no-frills, straight ahead and nonstop. He could knock out a man with either hand and did about half the time owning a 55 percent KO rate.

McGovern grew up in Brooklyn and never went to school. He worked a variety of jobs including one in a lumberyard. A boss saw him fight there and encouraged him to take up boxing. He turned pro in 1897 at age 17.

During their January 9, 1900 title bout, McGovern put Canada's George Dixon (Little Chocolate) down eight times in one round to win the featherweight belt. Dixon, who had ruled the feathers for 10 years, had never been knocked down before. McGovern became one of the few fighters up to that point to win titles in two classes. Before this fight he owned the bantamweight crown. He was outboxed by the skillful old pro for the first five rounds, but turned it on in the final three to gain the match and title at age 19.

McGovern fought lightweight champ Frank Ernie later the same year in a nontitle fight and knocked him out in three rounds (making him not quite a three-crown

Corbett called out, "Come on out, you Irish rat, and take the licking of your life!"

champ). In December he sort of defeated the mighty Joe Gans when the latter allegedly took a dive in the second round (Gans would go on to fight masterfully and legitimately to become a great lightweight champion and Hall of Famer.)

McGovern successfully defended his title six more times until he ran into Young Corbett in Hartford, Connecticut November 28, 1901. In a furious battle that lasted about a round and a half, Corbett finally rocked the champ with a right that put out the light.

Corbett went into this fight boldly and supremely savvy by rattling McGovern with taunts just before the fight started. In the dressing area Corbett called out, "Come on out, you Irish rat, and take the licking of your life!" McGovern took the bait and charged into the ring with murder on his mind. But he was was met with a fighter who didn't scare and gave better than he got.

Later in his career his behavior became erratic, and he spent time in sanitariums. During WWI he served as a referee in a U.S. Army camp and collapsed and died soon after.

McGovern was a gamer. Between his bouts with Dixon and Corbett, he had eight title fights plus eight nontitle, or 16 fights in 23 months. That's about one fight every six weeks.

Box Reg stats for Terry McGovern
RH, 5 foot 4 inches
Reach 65 inches
110-133 pounds
80 bouts, 4/1897 to 5/1908
Bantam champ 1899-1900
Feather champ 1900-1901
Hall of Fame 1990
Born 3/1880, Johnston, PA
Died 2/1918

Sources for Terry McGovern

boxrec.com

Casey, Mike. *Brooklyn's Finest: Terrible Terry McGovern,*
http://www.cyberboxingzone.com/boxing/casey/MC_McGovern.htm

Roberts, James B. and Skutt, Alexander G. *The Boxing Register.* Ithaca, New York: McBooks Press, Inc., 2011.

Sugar, Bert Randolph. *Boxing's Greatest Fighters.* Guilford, Connecticut: The Lyons Press, 2006.

Weston, Stanley and Farhood, Steven. *The Ring: Boxing The 20th Century.* New York: BDD Illustrated Books, 1993.

Willie Pep vs. Sandy Saddler

Abe Attell
The Little Hebrew
72-11-18, 39 KOs
154 total bouts

Abe Attell's ring moniker was (and this is absolutely truc) The Little Hebrew, a nod to the era's clumsy penchant to define all nonwhites as representatives of an ethnic group. But far from being offensive, most Jews at the time took a great deal of pride in their Jewish boxers who, after all, were just trying to get along and get ahead in America — so many were immigrants or sons of immigrants and saw boxing as a means to do so.

Attell won his first title in September 1903, lost it after two defenses in October 1904, won it back in February 1906 and had at least 20 successful defenses until February 1912, when he lost the title in his second fight with Johnny Kilbane. His string of defenses stood as a featherweight record well into the century.

Early on Attell chose a slugging style and in fact kayoed 24 of his first 28 opponents. But after watching boxers like James Corbett and George Dixon, he developed a more sophisticated set of skills that included slips, blocks and deft footwork. Thus he learned the art of boxing and incorporated into his style one of the great boxing maxims — *Hit the other guy more than he hits*

Not to be denied his winning KO and bet, Attell knocked out the manager and the ref was able to finish his count.

you. Because of his elusive, defensive style he was given another nickname, one that would be associated with Willie Pep a few years later — The Will o' the Wisp.

Attell was indeed a character.

He often bet on himself, which was not unusual at the time. He fought Freddie Weeks October 1907 and wagered that he would knock him out in the fourth round. Weeks went down in the fourth as planned, but as the referee counted him out, the fallen fighter's manager inexplicably stepped into the ring about to a cause a disruption. Not to be denied his winning KO and bet, Attell knocked out the manager, and the ref was able to finish his count. Attell bet $4,000 at 7-1 odds to win $28,000.

Attell lost his title to Johnny Kilbane in 1912. He had beaten Kilbane in 1910 in part because he trash talked throughout the bout and got into Kilbane's head. This time Kilbane talked back and won 19 out of 20 rounds. Kilbane almost swooned during a clinch in the 16th saying that there was chloroform on Attell's back. This claim was refuted by Attell's corner and never investigated.

Probably the most outlandish and troubling story regarding Abe Attell (outside the ring) was his friendship with Arnold Rothstein, the guy that allegedly fixed the

1919 World Series. As the story goes, Attell was the bagman, the fellow who gave the players $10,000 to throw the games. He was indited, but the charges were dropped for lack of evidence.

This intersection of gambling, gangsterism, boxing (in the person of Attell) and baseball is interesting and telling. From that point on, baseball cleaned itself up, organized and went on to enjoy a glorious decade and growth that transcended its raw beginnings to become our national pastime. Despite the efforts of the many, the good intentioned and the powerful, boxing never really eradicated the corrupt influence of gamblers, gangsters, hustlers and/or profiteers. And it never coalesced into an almighty entity like Major League Baseball.

Box Reg stats for Abe Attell
RH, 5 foot 4 inches
Reach 66 inches
116-133 pounds
154 bouts, 12/1900 to 1/1917
Feather champ 1901-1912
Hall of Fame 1990
Born 2/1884, San Francisco
Died 2/1970

Sources for Abe Attell

boxrec.com

International Boxing Hall of Fame, ibhof.com

Roberts, James B. and Skutt, Alexander G. *The Boxing Register.* Ithaca, New York: McBooks Press, Inc., 2011.

Sugar, Bert Randolph. *Boxing's Greatest Fighters.* Guilford, Connecticut: The Lyons Press, 2006.

Weston, Stanley and Farhood, Steven. *The Ring: Boxing The 20th Century.* New York: BDD Illustrated Books, 1993.

Willie Pep vs. Sandy Saddler

Jim Driscoll
Peerless Jim
58-3-6, 38 knockouts
77 total bouts

A true lightweight, Driscoll never fought above 126 pounds. Born Welsh, he cut his teeth working the British boxing booths — where a fighter would take on all comers. After hundreds(!) of such encounters, he turned pro in 1901 at age 21 and made his mark.

First he won the Welsh featherweight title, then the British version in 1906 and next the British Empire featherweight crown in 1908. American managers, Charley Harvey and Jimmy Johnston[1] (older brother of Charlie Johnston who would be Sandy Saddler's manager), brought him to the United States that same year. Story goes they met him at the dock, but doubted this scrawny fellow with the swollen ears could be the British champion. Johnston threw a few punches and Driscoll deftly slipped each one by 1/16 inch. Welcome to America!

During that first American trip he enjoyed a string of victories that included a 10-round drubbing of featherweight champion Abe Attell in New York City. Although officially a no-decision (because the fight did not end in a KO[2]), by all accounts Driscoll dominated. Himself unmarked, Attell's eye was closed and his nose swollen at the finish. This fight established his reputation in America and prompted local newsman and ex-gunslinger Bat Masterson to give him his lasting ring name — Peerless Jim.

This fight estab-lished his reputa-tion in America and prompted local newsman and ex-gunslinger Bat Masterson to give him his lasting ring name — Peerless Jim.

Back across the Atlantic, Driscoll won the British and European feather-weight titles and retired for the first time in 1912 an undefeated cham-pion. He served in the Army during World War I and made a comeback in 1919. In his third fight he lost by a TKO (the only time he was stopped) and retired for good.

He suffered from tuber-culosis and died from pneumonia in 1925.

He was known for his cauliflower ears. Perhaps because of those slight slips of 1/16 inch — enough for a punch to miss the head, but not his protruding ears.

He was a quick and elusive boxer. But he had great hand speed and good power — garnering 38 KOs in 77 bouts. Driscoll was one of those select fighters whose ring prowess elicited comments like "perfection," "artistry," "a revelation."

He founded the Driscoll School of Boxing.

Notes in text

1 Promoter/manager Jimmy Johnson was known as the Boy Bandit — one of boxing history's most colorful figures. Besides Driscoll, he and Harvey imported other English fighters like Hall of Famers Owen Moran and Ted "Kid" Lewis. His promotions included the serious and the outlandish. He staged three heavyweight title fights "in which the belt changed hands" and numerous "stunts" including midget boxing matches. (From *The Boxing Register*, page 870)

2 In the early years of the century, if no fighter was knocked out after the final bell, the match was rendered a no-decision — no winner, no loser. It was thought that if only a KO could decide a match, the chance for illicit influence (from gamblers) would be mitigated.

Box Reg stats for Jim Driscoll
RH, 5 foot 6 inches
Reach (none given)
120-126 pounds
77 bouts, 1901 to 10/1919
EBU and Brit World Feather Champ 1912-13
Hall of Fame 1990
Born 12/1880, Cardiff, Wales
Died 1/1925

Sources for Jim Driscoll

boxrec.com

Roberts, James B. and Skutt, Alexander G. *The Boxing Register*. Ithaca, New York: McBooks Press, Inc., 2011.

Sugar, Bert Randolph. *Boxing's Greatest Fighters*. Guilford, Connecticut: The Lyons Press, 2006.

Weston, Stanley and Farhood, Steven. *The Ring: Boxing The 20th Century*. New York: BDD Illustrated Books, 1993.

Willie Pep vs. Sandy Saddler

Johnny Kilbane
48-5-7, 25 KOs
142 total bouts

In some ways Johnny Kilbane was an opposite of the boxer he beat to gain the light-weight title February 1912. Abe Attell was a rough and ready customer. He took on everybody, fought prolifically and was not afraid to play out-side the lines. Kilbane was a straight arrow (compared to Attell) and even held public office.

He was a boxer's boxer and happy to outpoint an oppo-nent. Perhaps his greatest fight, Kilbane dominated Attell over 20 rounds with a relentless jab that eventually closed Attell's left eye. Kilbane frustrated the Little Hebrew so much with his evasive footwork and head movement that Attell resorted to heeling, butting and elbowing, but to no avail.

Kilbane held the title for a record 11 years (1912-1923) and defended it a somewhat modest 10 times (averaging less than once a year), a fact critics of his reign will point out. His ring skills, in his prime, were unassailable. He was commonly described as a scientific boxer — intelli-gent, very fast, quick on his feet and able to avoid punches. This most probably sustained his longevity and mental acuity after he left the ring. He became a state senator, which of course, is solid proof that he remained clearheaded into middle age.

Kilbane had not fought for two years when he met the French champion, Eugene Criqui, in 1923. It is said he was paid $75,0000 to show up. What also showed was the results of inactivity and age. He got punched about and knocked out in the 6th.

The Frenchman, by the way, was a study in courage and toughness. He was shot in the face during WWI and his jaw shattered. Doctors told him his fighting days were over, but a successful surgery and recovery encouraged Criqui to climb back into the ring and eventually become champion. The story goes that his jaw was fixed with wire, metal plates and a sheep's rib.

Kilbaned his peeper

Kilbane was champion for a long time. Long enough for his name to become a verb during his decade-plus reign. If a fellow were to clobber another fellow, you might say that the first guy "Kilbaned" the second. Here's a colorful sampling of the usage in *The New York Times:*

Everything was very pleasant at the Detroit-Yankee game on the Hilltop yesterday until Ty Cobb johnnykilbaned a spectator right on the place where he talks, started the claret, and stopped the flow of profane and vulgar words. Cobb led with a left jab and countered with a right kick to Mr. Spectator's left Welsbach, which made his peeper look as if some one had drawn a curtain over it.[1]

Box Reg stats for Johnny Kilbane

RH, 5 foot 5 inches
Reach 68 inches
120 1/2-133 pounds
142 bouts, 12/1907 to 6/1923
Feather champ 1912-1923
Hall of Fame 1995
Born 4/1889, Cleveland, OH
Died 5/1957

Sources for Johnny Kilbane

boxrec.com

The New York Times

Roberts, James B. and Skutt, Alexander G. The Boxing Register. Ithaca, New York: McBooks Press, Inc., 2011.

Sugar, Bert Randolph. Boxing's Greatest Fighters. Guilford, Connecticut: The Lyons Press, 2006.

Weston, Stanley and Farhood, Steven. The Ring: Boxing The 20th Century. New York: BDD Illustrated Books, 1993.

Footnote for this section

1 "Cobb Whips Hilltop Fan for Insults," The New York Times, 16 May 1912.

Willie Pep vs. Sandy Saddler

Johnny Dundee
The Scotch Wop
88-32-20, 22 KOs
341 total bouts
(Over 3,000 rounds!)

Here's another ring name for the books — The Scotch Wop. And he was hardly a Scotsman. Johnny Dundce was born Giuseppe Carrora, November 1893 in Sicily. His manager thought his real name sounded more like a vegetable, so Dundee it was.

His claim to fame is endurance. He fought 341 times over a span of 21 years, from 1910 to 1932. He had 47 bouts in 1911 alone (losing only once)!

He was known for his "ring trickery and dazzling footwork," and being "adept at launching punches while bouncing off the ropes."[1] He outboxed most of his opponents — his knockout percentage was a paltry seven percent. He was KO'd just once.

His family ran a fishmarket in New York City's Hell's Kitchen. He was a street fighter until discovered and groomed by Scotty Monteith. Never an amateur, he turned pro at 16, starting out as a bantam.

In 1913 he fought featherweight champ Kilbane to a 20-round draw, but observers gave the edge to Dundee. He

He had 47 bouts in 1911 alone (losing only once)!

fought legendary lightweight Benny Leonard eight times between 1915 and 1920, all no decisions — but newspapers said Dundee won three of those fights.

He won the first ever junior lightweight championship in 1921 versus George KO Chaney on a foul. He won the New York World Featherweight Championship by defeating Danny Frush in 1922. He lost and regained the junior lightweight title against Jack Bernstein in 1923. Between those fights he took on Eugene Criqui, the generally accepted featherweight champ, and won in front of 40,000 fans.

Dundee lost most of his ring earnings on a poor stable of race horses.

Box Reg stats for Johnny Dundee
RH, 5 foot 4 1/2 inches
Reach 63 inches
105-135 pounds
341 bouts, 8/1910 to 12/1932
Junior Light Champ 1921-23, 1923-24
NY World Feather Champ 1922-23
Feather Champ 1923-24
Hall of Fame 1991
Born 11/1893, Sciacca, Sicily, Italy
Died 4/1965

Sources for Johnny Dundee

Fleischer, Nate and Andre, Sam. *An Illustrated History of Boxing.* Secaucus, New Jersey: Carol Publishing Group, 1997.

Roberts, James B. and Skutt, Alexander G. *The Boxing Register.* Ithaca, New York: McBooks Press, Inc., 2011.

Sugar, Bert Randolph. *Boxing's Greatest Fighters.* Guilford, Connecticut: The Lyons Press, 2006.

Footnote for this section

1 James B. Roberts and Alexander G. Skutt, *The Boxing Register* (Ithaca: McBooks Press, Inc., 2011), 122.

Willie Pep vs. Sandy Saddler

Canzoneri took on the very best of his time — he had 36 bouts with 18 world champs, defeating 15.

Tony Canzoneri
Canzi
137-24-10, 44 KOs
175 total bouts

The Italian American legend known as Canzi was born November 1908 in Louisiana, but raised in New York City. He became New York State Amateur Champion in 1924. Later that year he began to fight professionally.

Canzi won the featherweight title in February 1928 — the youngest featherweight champ ever — at age 19. He defeated Benny Bass in a 15-round decision.

In November 1930 he KO'd Al Singer in the first round to win the lightweight championship. It was the fastest KO in lightweight title bout history — 66 seconds.

In April 1931 Canzoneri won the junior welterweight crown by defeating Kid Berg with a third round knockout. With this win and title he became one of the very few triple-crown winners in boxing history.

Canzi was both a puncher and a boxer and became a huge crowd favorite toward the end of his career. Canzoneri took on the very best of his time — he had 36 bouts with 18 world champs, defeating 15. He fought in 22 championship bouts in his 10 peak years.

He was KO'd only once — in his last fight.

After fighting he invested in Broadway shows, had a nightclub act and operated a restaurant.

Box Reg stats for Tony Canzoneri
RH, 5 foot 5 inches
Reach 65 inches
117-144 pounds
175 bouts, 7/1925 to 11/1939
Feather Champ 1927-28
Light Champ 1930-33, 1935-36
Junior Welt Champ 1931-32, 1933
Hall of Fame 1990
Born 11/1908, Slidell, LA
Died 12/1959

Sources for Tony Canzoneri

Roberts, James B. and Skutt, Alexander G. *The Boxing Register.* Ithaca, New York: McBooks Press, Inc., 2011.

Sugar, Bert Randolph. *Boxing's Greatest Fighters.* Guilford, Connecticut: The Lyons Press, 2006.

"The people thought I cried because I was happy to win the title. I was crying because my hands hurt."

Battling Battalino
Bat
58-26-3, 23 KOs
88 total fights

Christopher Battalino was born in Hartford, Connecticut (Willie Pep's neck of the woods) in 1908.

In his early years he was known for his "great speed and punching power."

Bat was the son of immigrant parents and never went to high school. He worked in a typewriter factory and on tobacco fields around Hartford. Johnny Dundee was his hero. He was working out in a local gym by 1925 and fought as an amateur in 1926 and 1927 — winning the Connecticut featherweight title both years. He became the 1927 National AAU (Amateur Athletic Union) featherweight champion and turned pro later that year.

In September 1929 Battalino defeated Frenchman Andre Routis in Hartford to gain the featherweight championship in front of 25,000 fans. In that fight he broke both hands in the fourth round, but went on to win a 15-round decision. Afterward he said, "The people thought I cried because I was happy to win the title. I was crying because my hands hurt."[1]

Battalino fought Kid Chocolate in 1930 at Madison Square Garden. He was knocked down by the first punch of the fight, but pursued the Kid thereafter. He attacked the body, while the Kid countered to his head. It was close, but Battalino took the decision and earned $25,000 — his biggest payday.

In January 1932, he faced Freddie Miller. The contest was stopped in the third round because, as the referee saw it, Battalino failed to put up a fight. So he was stripped of the belt and gave up all claims to the title to move up to lightweight. In an interview years later, Battalino claimed he threw the fight.

As one reporter saw things, Battalino was "Possessed of little boxing ability, but capable of taking up to five socks to get in one good one ... His forte is ceaseless body punching ..."[2]

He worked construction in Hartford after fighting.

Box Reg stats for Battling Battalino
RH, 5 foot 5 inches
Reach 65 inches
123 1/2-146 1/2 pounds
88 bouts, 6/1927 to 1/1940
Feather Champ 1929-32
Hall of Fame 2003
Born 2/1908, Hartford, CT
Died 7/1977

Sources for Battling Battalino
Heller, Peter. *"In This Corner ...!"* New York, New York: Da Capo Press, 1994.

The Reading Eagle

Footnotes for this section
1 Peter Heller. *"In This Corner ...!"* (New York: Da Capo Press, 1994), 144.
2 "Barney Ross Tackles Bat Battalino Tonight," *The Reading Eagle*, 21 October 1932.

And here's the fact of facts on this busy gentleman — he boxed 2,028 rounds.

Freddie Miller
203-32-8, 45 KOs
252 total bouts

Freddie Miller was born in Cincinnati in April 1911 and fought professionally from 1927 to 1940. He was what they called an "active" fighter. Miller had 75 fights before he was 19. Turning pro in 1927, he had 30 professional fights in his first year, losing only four. That's more than two fights each month!

In all, Miller had a remarkable 252 fights — winning 203, losing 32 with eight draws. And here's the fact of facts on this busy gentleman — he boxed 2,028 rounds. After 13 years he retired at the wizened age of 28.

In 1931 Miller had his first title fight with then featherweight champ Bat Battalino in Cincinnati and lost by a decision. Six months later he fought him again, but Battalino apparently threw the fight, and the bout was declared a no decision. As a result, Bat was stripped of the title and Miller was dropped from *The Ring* magazine's annual rankings.

Miller did not blow his second chance and defeated Tommy Paul for the National Boxing Association (NBA) world featherweight title in Chicago in 1933. And then beat Nel Tarleton in Liverpool, England in 1934 to become undisputed featherweight champion.

Miller successfully defended his world featherweight

title a respectable 12 times. At one stretch he defended the title five times in three years. He fought 48 nontitle fights and won 41.

Miller lost the title to Petey Sarron in May 1937 although he had beaten Sarron thrice before. They fought a non-title bout in Johannesburg, South Africa in July of that year. Miller won, but lost the title match in the same town two months later. It was the first time two Americans fought for a championship outside the United States.

He was something of a featherweight ambassador to the world (like Sandy Saddler was to become). Miller fought in more than 12 nations including England, Scotland, Spain, France, Ireland, Mexico, Cuba, Belgium, South Africa, Wales and Venezuela. Miller also fought in most every major American city.

Miller was not a slugger — his KO percentage was under 18 percent. He won on points with reflexes and hand speed. His lefty stance posed problems for most — he was difficult to hurt and almost impossible to stop.

Miller suffered a KO only once — in his last fight.

Box Reg stats for Freddie Miller
LH, 5 foot 5 inches
Reach 65 1/2 inches
122 1/2-131 pounds
252 bouts, 4/1927 to 4/1940
NBA Feather Champ 1933-34
World Feather Champ 1934-36
Hall of Fame 1997
Born 4/1911, Cincinnati, OH
Died 5/1962

Sources for Freddie Miller

boxrec.com

The Cincinnati Herald

eastsideboxing.com

Roberts, James B. and Skutt, Alexander G. *The Boxing Register.* Ithaca, New York: McBooks Press, Inc., 2011.

Willie Pep vs. Sandy Saddler

They sat through every feature and saw how Gans threw a jab, Johnson tied up his man and Leonard moved his feet.

Kid Chocolate
132-10-6, 50 KOs
149 total bouts

Owner of one of the greatest ring names in boxing history, Kid Chocolate was born Eligio Sardinias y Montalbo in Cerro, Cuba. A colorful and much admired character in and out of the ring in the late 1920s and early 1930s, he became the first Cuban to win a world title. Chocolate also went as the Cuban Bon Bon, and of course, the Kid.

He was discovered and coached in Havana by a newspaper man who took him to the movies to study newsreels of Joe Gans, Jack Johnson and Benny Leonard — boxing heros of the day. They sat through every feature and saw how Gans threw a jab, Johnson tied up his man and Leonard moved his feet. Together they molded a fighter who is said to have won 100 straight amateur fights, but that may be inflated from a more reasonable 23.

Somewhat tall for a lighter fighter (at 5 feet 6 inches) he owned a reach that may have been 68 inches — some reach for a feather or lightweight (shades of things to come with one Sandy Saddler, another Caribbean transplant).

A hugely popular figure, his fight with Al Singer drew

45,000, the largest ever for a nontitle fight in the lighter classes up to that time (Singer was World Lightweight Champion in 1930).

Further indication of his success is found in a newspaper headline that said "Kid Chocolate Earns $75,000 for Half-Hour's Work." This caught the eye of a young Henry Armstrong, who would become boxing's only simultaneous triple-crown champ. He quit his job pounding railroad spikes and told friends if a Cuban could make that kind of scratch, so could a hungry American.

Sugar Ray Robinson was said to be an admirer and incorporated elements of his style.

Chocolate is remembered for his flashy style and boxing ability. The Kid developed a strong left jab and an array of defensive skills based on fleet feet and head and body movement. He was accomplished at fighting from range or inside and a master counterpuncher. Sugar Ray Robinson was said to be an admirer and incorporated elements of his style.

A very busy and accomplished professional, he fought eight world champions and won his first 51 professional fights without a loss before losing a split decision to Kid Berg in front of 40,000 fans. Among his greatest fights were controversial losses to Battling Battalino for the World Featherweight Title, Tony Canzoneri for the World Lightweight Title and aforementioned Kid Berg — all Hall of Fame boxers.

Why controversial? In all three bouts the crowd roared its disapproval with the decisions. James P. Dawson of *The New York Times* had Chocolate over Battalino nine rounds out of 15, although some ringsiders saw a "listless" Kid. Canzoneri, the local boy, was booed for 10 minutes, even though his attack in later rounds probably won him the decision. "A storm of protest" went up after the victory was handed to Berg, but the latter also staged an impressive offensive performance that was said to tire Chocolate.

He did win the Junior Lightweight Title in 1931 and the NYSAC (New York State Athletic Commission) World Featherweight title in 1932.

The story goes that he loved the nightlife during his fighting days in the United States and contracted syphilis, but apparently was successfully treated. He moved back to Cuba, lived a quite life there and, although ignored by Castro's Cuba at first, eventually was honored with a small pension. He died at 78.

Box Reg stats for Kid Chocolate
RH, 5 foot 6 inches
Reach 65 inches
118-133 pounds
149 bouts, 2/1928 to 12/1938
Junior Feather Champ 1931-33
NY World Feather Champ 1932-34
Hall of Fame 1991
Born 1/1910, Cierro, Cuba
Died 8/1958

Sources for Kid Chocolate

boxrec.com

http://coxscorner.tripod.com/chocolate.html

Roberts, James B. and Skutt, Alexander G. *The Boxing Register.* Ithaca, New York: McBooks Press, Inc., 2011.

Sugar, Bert Randolph. *Boxing's Greatest Fighters.* Guilford, Connecticut: The Lyons Press, 2006.

Weston, Stanley and Farhood, Steven. *The Ring: Boxing The 20th Century.* New York: BDD Illustrated Books, 1993.

Henry Armstrong
Homicide Hank,
Hammerin Hank
150-21-9, 101 KOs
180 total bouts

The Henry Armstrong story is a utterly remarkable — humble beginnings, overwhelming odds, soaring success, epic accomplishment and a slow, wretched decline. Armstrong was arguably the greatest of them all. In an era that had only eight weight classes, he held three titles at the same time — a feat never duplicated.

Hammerin Hank owned a hard punch and killer attitude. Tough as nails and die hard, he fought with a relentless bob and weave to get inside his man. His fierce infighting ability overcame an inferior reach and enabled him to dismantle most opponents, even the larger, heavier ones.

Armstrong was the 11th of 15 children. His father was a farmer and butcher, a mix of Native American, Irish and African American ancestry. His mother, with the storybook name America, was half Cherokee. The family moved to St. Louis when he was 4 and his mother died one year later. He was raised by a grandmother.

As a boy he dreamed about becoming a doctor. About

the time he graduated from high school, his father died and he felt compelled to work for the Missouri-Pacific Railroad in order to help provide for his family. He ran 10 miles to work each morning even though a rail car was available — then he pounded spikes for hours on end. He enjoyed the hard labor in part because he understood that Jack Dempsey once did the same thing.

What could rival the epic feats of the Brown Bomber? They could try to win three titles, that's what.

It happened one day that a wind blown newspaper landed at his feet displaying a headline that said the great boxer, Kid Chocolate, had earned $75,000 for half hour's work. That was the spark that ignited his swelling ambition. He said if the Cuban could do it, so could he. Young Henry took to street fighting, discovered the gyms and started boxing as an amateur.

In 1931 he tried boxing as a pro in the Pittsburgh area with limited success. He fought using his real name, Henry Jackson. He soon relocated to Los Angeles, changed his name to Henry Armstrong to cover his brief stint as a pro and resumed his amateur career — winning 85 fights while operating a shoe shine parlor. Armstrong turned pro after failing to make the 1932 Olympic boxing team.

By 1934, Armstrong was a feature attraction in Los

Angeles. His first major fight was with Baby Arizmendi in Mexico City where he may have been robbed of a decision by hometown judges. Another match in January 1935 yielded the same result. Finally he won a third fight with Arizmendi in Los Angeles in August 1936 to gain the California/Mexico version of the featherweight crown (Armstrong would go on to beat Arizmendi in two more battles).

As luck would have it, Hollywood star Al Jolson saw the third Arizmendi fight and bought his contract. Jolson's frontman, Eddie Meade, proved an excellent manager and got Armstrong fights with good fighters and there followed a spectacular 24 months of boxing. In 1937 Armstrong could not be beat, winning all 27 of his fights — 26 by knockout. That's a fight (and a victory) every two weeks!

Along in there came the Big Idea. The brain trust of Jolson, Meade and later George Raft (another Hollywood celeb) knew they had a great fighter, but his success was greatly overshadowed by Joe Louis, the wildly popular heavyweight champion. What could they do with their smaller fighter? What could rival the epic feats of the Brown Bomber? They could try to win three titles, that's what. Armstrong could not compete with Joe Louis's popularity straight on, but to win title after title after title would certainly reap reward. In October 1937 Armstrong knocked out Petey Sarron for the featherweight title — one down, two to go.

As great as Armstrong was in 1937, 1938 was his greatest year. In May he defeated Barney Ross for the welterweight title at Madison Square Garden in front of

28,290. He gave Ross a 15-round beating that should have been stopped.

For this title fight Armstrong had to add weight to appease the New York State Athletic Commission (NYSAC). They demanded that he weigh at least 138 pounds. Since he was naturally lighter at the time, tipping the scales at 126, he had to drink glass after glass of water on the day of the weigh-in and fight. Fortunately, the bout was postponed after the weigh-in, so Armstrong was able to relieve the bloating.

One fighter went down, the other way up. By the time of the fight Armstrong weighed 133 and Ross 160. Despite the discrepancy, Homicide Hank overwhelmed the older champion and actually carried him the last four rounds. After the bout Armstrong said, "I was asked to do it, and he [Ross] thanked me for it."

Then he fought Lou Ambers for the lightweight title. Armstrong knocked Ambers down in the fifth and sixth rounds. But Ambers cut Armstrong's eyes and mouth and the referee considered stopping the fight. Armstrong discarded his mouthpiece so he could swallow the blood from his mouth cut (so it would not pour to the canvas) and won a split decision. He now owned featherweight, lightweight and welterweight titles — perhaps the most impressive accomplishment in ring history.

Armstrong relinquished the featherweight title in 1938 because he could no longer make weight. He lost the lightweight title to Ambers in a return match in 1939 after the referee took five(!) rounds from Hammerin Hank for low blows. But over the next few months he defended his welterweight title a truly impressive 19 times — 11 times in 1939.

In 1937 Armstrong could not be beat, winning all 27 of his fights — 26 by knockout. That's a fight (and a victory) every two weeks!

In March 1940 he fought middleweight champ Ceferino Garcia to a draw. It is said that he was offered $75,000 to take a dive, but refused. At least one historian, Bert Sugar, says Armstrong won the title bout with Garcia, but that the draw was "one of boxing's little pre-arrangements ..."[1]

Later that year he lost the welterweight title to Fritzie Zivic and could not beat him in a rematch. He finally beat him in their third meeting, but Zivic was not a champ at the time.

Armstrong stayed in the ring until 1945. In retirement, he financed a movie about himself, *Keep Punching*, opened a bar in Los Angeles and marketed a remedy for arthritis. He became an alcoholic, but in time managed to stop drinking and was ordained a Baptist minister in 1951. He returned to St Louis, founded The Henry Armstrong Youth Foundation and directed The Herbert Hoover Boys Club.

Armstrong's lifetime earnings may have amounted to a million dollars, but there was little to show in the end.

He and his wife lived on a monthly social security check of $800. He was to suffer at various times pneumonia, anemia, cataracts, malnutrition and dementia. He died in Los Angeles at 75.

Box Reg stats for Henry Armstrong

RH, 5 foot 5 1/2 inches
Reach 67 inches
120-148 pounds
180 bouts, 7/1931 to 2/1945
Feather Champ 1937-38
Light Champ 1938-39
Welt Champ 1938-40
Hall of Fame 1990
Born 12/1912, Columbus, MS
Died 10/1988

Sources for Henry Armstrong

Roberts, James B. and Skutt, Alexander G. *The Boxing Register.* Ithaca, New York: McBooks Press, Inc., 2011.

Sugar, Bert Randolph. *Boxing's Greatest Fighters.* Guilford, Connecticut: The Lyons Press, 2006.

Weston, Stanley and Farhood, Steven. *The Ring: Boxing The 20th Century.* New York: BDD Illustrated Books, 1993.

Footnote for this section

1 Bert Randolph Sugar, *Boxing's Greatest Fighters* (Gilford: The Lyons Press, 2006), 5.

His was a long road to glory — it took 13 years and 140 fights before winning the championship.

Albert Wright
Chalky
158-43-18, 81 KOs,
221 total bouts

Chalky Wright is an interesting study and maybe a little underappreciated.

Sometimes described as tall for a feather, he may have been 5 foot 7 1/2 inches (some records show an inch shorter). He had a long reach for a small fighter, 69 inches, which served him well at range (as it would Sandy Saddler). Wright could hit hard and he knew how to box. He had some ups and downs before he hit paydirt (and some interesting sidebars), but he hung in there, fought champions and became a champion in a career that lasted 20 years.

His was a long road to glory — it took 13 years and 140 fights before winning the championship.

He may have been born in February 1912, but this is disputed. His place of birth is also disputed — Durango, Colorado or Durango, Mexico or Willcox, Arizona. His grandfather may have been a runaway slave. Perhaps his family included black cowboys.

It is said his family worked as migrant farm workers. His father left soon after he was born, and his mother moved her brood to Los Angeles. His first pro bout was in 1928 at age 16. Fighting in California exclusively, he had a record of 48-7-1 during the first five years. Over the next five years Wright fought less and worked as a driver for movie legend Mae West. There are stories that he also served as her bodyguard and lover. His record at this point was 0-6 against ranked fighters. He fought bantam weight contenders Newboy Brown and Pablo Dano, ex-champ Baby Arizmendi, featherweight contender Al Reid and the ferocious Henry Armstrong.

"... he is the greatest boxer and smartest operator and the most efficient puncher of his time ..."

Then came a big break. He was hired by Henry Armstrong to be a sparring partner for an upcoming fight with Barney Ross. Manager Eddie Walker liked what he saw and added Wright to his collection of boxers. With this mighty team on his side, he started winning again. He eventually was ranked sixth-best feather by *The Ring Magazine*, one of the prominent deciders of such things.

By 1938 Wright was taking fights on the East Coast and the boxing world took notice. In 1941 he defeated future champ Sal Bartolo and "secured a title fight." In September 1941 he KO'd featherweight champion Joey Archibald in the 11th round. Within a month he fought nontitle bouts with Jose Peralta (loss) and former champ Leo Rodak (win). In 1942 he KO'd future champ Richie Lemos and won title matches with ex-champ Harry Jaffra and Lulu Constantino.

Then he met Willie Pep at year's end and lost the title. Despite the lopsided decision in Pep's favor, not all at ringside were impressed with Wee Willie's first victory over Wright. Reporter Dick McCann of the *New York Daily News* said that Pep retreated "faster and more frequently than Rommel's Afrika Corps."[1] He scored the fight for Wright.

Columnist Frank Graham said, "There is, in short, little to distinguish (Pep) from a dozen other featherweights."[2]

Wright continued to impress "schooled observers"[3] in the bouts that came after. On June 6, 1943 reporter Stanley Woodward of the *New York Tribune* had glowing words for Wright's performance against Phil Terranova: "... he is the greatest boxer and smartest operator and the most efficient puncher of his time ..."[4]

In the 1944 rematch, Wright was once more defeated by Pep. This fight is a bit of history in that it was the first televised bout sponsored by the Gillette Safety Razor Company. *The Gillette Friday Night Fights* would become extremely popular and among the era's most watched programs. He lost to Pep again two months later (and a fourth time in November 1946). Wright fought on for a few years, but the warrior was on the wane, and he lost nine of his last 10 fights.

To his lasting credit, Wright took on all comers including lightweights and welterweights. Boxing historian Hank Kaplan said he was "a good all-around boxer-puncher."[5] He knew how to move and could take out his man — after all, he knocked out 81 opponents.

The thing is, he ran into a Willie Pep who was in his prime.

Wright left the ring in 1948. Retirement was dismal. Most of his earnings were gambled away. He found work in a bakery, left his wife and moved in with his mother. Wright died after slipping in a bathtub in August 1957.

He was 45 years old.

Box Reg stats for Chalky Wright
RH, 5 foot 7 1/2 inches
Reach 69 inches
120-136 pounds
221 bouts, 2/1928 to 3/1948
Feather Champ 1941-42
Hall of Fame 1997
Born 2/1912, Durango, CO (date and place disputed)
Died 8/1957

Sources for Chalky Wright

boxrec.com

cyberboxing.com

International Boxing Hall of Fame, ibhof.com

Roberts, James B. and Skutt, Alexander G. *The Boxing Register.* Ithaca, New York: McBooks Press, Inc., 2011.

Sports Illustrated

Weston, Stanley and Farhood, Steven. *The Ring: Boxing The 20th Century.* New York: BDD Illustrated Books, 1993.

Footnotes for this section

1 Stanley Weston and Steven Farhood, *The Ring: Boxing The 20th Century* (New York: BDD Illustrated Books, 1993), 72.
2 Ibid.
3 James B. Roberts and Alexander G. Skutt, *The Boxing Register* (Ithaca: McBooks Press, Inc., 2011), 793.
4 Ibid.
5 Ibid.

Extreme measures for extreme times

The Works Progress Administration (WPA) was the largest jobs initiative in U.S history — President Franklin Roosevelt's answer to the monstrous unemployment that plagued the nation during the 1930s. The WPA was a monumental reaction to the almost incom-

prehensible misery that was felt nationwide and worldwide. Unemployment stood at nearly 25 percent of the American work force in 1933. Millions were in dire straits — homeless, hungry, with hardly more than the clothes on their backs.

From 1935 through 1943 the program employed more than 8.5 million people working for an average salary of just under $42 a month. They rebuilt a nation's aging, decaying infrastructure with new roads, bridges, water and sewage treatment systems, hospitals, schools, airports and national parks. Programs also included slum clearance, reforestation and rural rehabilitation. Special programs included work for writers, artists, musicians and those in the theater.

During its 8-year history, the WPA built 651,087 miles of highways, roads and streets. The program constructed, repaired or improved 124,031 bridges, 125,110 public buildings, 8,192 parks and 853 airport landing fields, hospitals and schools.

The WPA touched almost every American life. And although it had (and has still) vociferous critics, it is widely believed that the federal program held the country together through one of its most trying times.

Sources for this article

"More About the WPA," The Lilly Library,
http://www.indiana.edu/~liblilly/wpa/wpa_info.html

"The Works Progress Administration (WPA)," PBS,
http://www.pbs.org/wgbh/americanexperience/features/general-article/dust-bowl-wpa/

"Works Progress Administration," *The New York Times*,
http://topics.nytimes.com/top/reference/timestopics/organizations/w/works_progress_administration/index.html?8qa

3. Early Pep

"I was a scrappy kid that they tried to push around ... I didn't know anything about boxing then. I was just a kid, but I knew enough not to get hit."

Getting by

Willie Pep was born William Guiglermo Papaleo on September 9, 1922, in Middletown, Connecticut, near the city of Hartford. He was the son of Italian immigrants — Salvatore and Mary Papaleo. As Willie would say, "My parents were from the other side." To be precise, the couple came from the ancient city of Syracuse, Sicily. They couldn't speak a word of English and their new life wasn't easy, although much better than the life they left behind.

His father worked construction. When the Great Depression took hold he was lucky to find work with the WPA (Works Progress Administration) earning $15 a week. These were trying times. (See previous page.)

Fighting for his turf
William did his part by working as a shoeshine boy. It was as a shoeshine boy that he began to fight — in order to protect his corner from competition. He was tough and tried to stand his ground, but sometimes he got whipped by bigger boys. Although this never kept him from getting back up.

"When you're in the ring, make believe a cop is chasing you; don't let him catch you."

Regarding his corner, "I was an 11-year-old kid. Back then, you had to get there early because it was a good spot. If you got there late, somebody would take your spot."[1]

He had his work cut out for him. "I weighed about 89 pounds soaking wet. The big guys would pick on me and so I had to fight them. Once you fight them they will leave you alone."[2]

He learned to avoid punches (his signature trait as a champion) even back then. "I was a scrappy kid that they tried to push around, but I wouldn't let them. I didn't know anything about boxing then. I was just a kid, but I knew enough not to get hit."[3]

"You're a Sucker"
Papa Guglielmo took his boy to a fight or two. William saw heavyweight champ Primo Carnera in an exhibition bout in 1930 and watched featherweight champion and Hartford hero Battling Battalino in training. But the boy's street fighting was less in pursuit of a boxing career than simply surviving (or having fun) until he was stopped by a witness to one of his fights who said, "You ought to be ashamed of yourself. You're a sucker. Why fight on the street for free when you can get eight dollars for the same thing in the gym?"[4]

The boy took the advice, found a gym that would teach

him the finer points, and it was game on for about 30 years. "The best advice I ever got," said Pep, "was from a kid in the gym who told me, 'When you're in the ring, make believe a cop is chasing you; don't let him catch you.'"[5]

Fighting for fun and profit
The local club, the Du-well Gym, didn't exactly greet the young fighter with open arms. He was initially turned down because of his size. He returned with the requisite head gear (and moxie) and finally got in the door. This was around 1938. He was 15 years old. "I got knocked down nine times a day, but I learned. I was determined."[6]

William began fighting as an amateur and made eight or nine dollars a match (Connecticut allowed its amateur boxers to earn). He brought the money home to Mom and Dad and got a buck in return.

One night he won the wondrous sum of $50.

He put $10 in his shoe and handed over the rest of his winnings to Mom who worried about the size of the new amount. "Maybe he did something wrong," she said to her husband. Pop took the boy aside and asked him about the money. Willie said it was all from the boxing. His father gave him two dollars and said he should try to fight twice a week.

Now $50 was a lot of money in 1940. It had the same buying power as $800 in 2012. While Papa was making $15 a week, young William's payouts from boxing, even at the lessor amount of eight dollars, must have seemed heaven-sent. His career path would never suffer parental obstruction.

He won 19 straight bouts before losing to one Angelo Randano. This is some streak considering young Will was so small and light. At 109 pounds, he was about 15 pounds lighter than most of the other boys. Despite the handicap he won another 19 straight, dropped a decision to Ray Robinson (yes, *that* Ray Robinson), then lost his third and last amateur decision to Earl Roys in the final round of the Connecticut State Amateur Flyweight Championship in 1937. However, he would win that title the following year. In 1939 he won the state amateur bantamweight crown.

Fighting Sugar Ray way back when
His amateur fight with Sugar Ray Robinson is one of those juicy nuggets of boxing history. Who knew that these two boys would one day compete for pound-for-pound greatness?

Pep recalled the meeting with his usual self-effacement and sense of humor:

"I was a flyweight and he was a featherweight. At that time I had a manager from Hartford, he was the bravest manager in the world. He didn't care who I fought. He put me in with a fellow that weighed 20 pounds more. If I weighed the same amount, maybe I couldn't beat Ray. I had no business being in the same ring with Ray that night. He was a great amateur fighter."[7]

Buster is a bust
His first manager is simply referred to as Buster in Pep's book, *Friday's Heros* (apparently he doesn't rate a last

"I got knocked down nine times a day, but I learned. I was determined." name or Pep is sparing someone the embarrassment). At any rate, Buster was cheap. He fed him donuts and coffee for breakfast and scrambled eggs for dinner. Young William didn't know the difference. He ate crackers and milk at home.

It was Buster who put him against Rodano and Robinson. In the former bout, Pep knocked Rodano down in the first round, but got knocked down nine times over the next three rounds. Pep would remember the Robinson encounter in the present tense, "He's all over me. He's too good. Too big. He's punching me and punching me and I'm just trying to hang in there."[8]

William eventually made a management change, his only one, when he came under the wings of trainer Bill Gore and manager Lou Viscusi.

1938 was the year of the great name change. Needing a moniker that had punch, he decided to call himself Willie Pep (against Pop's wishes).

Never was there a more apt name.

Four rounds for $15, 10 rounds for $20,000

At 17 Pep was a four-round fighter without a fight. With two friends he left the East Coast and went to California. They drove Route 66 all the way and landed at the Main Street Gym in Los Angeles — broke and hungry. Pep scored a sparring gig with a Manuel Ortiz for a dollar a

Pop took the boy aside and asked him about the money. Willie said it was all from the boxing. His father gave him two dollars and said he should try to fight twice a week.

round. Ortiz was bantamweight champ at the time. He boxed him three rounds a day for a week. Pep would say, "That three dollars a day was our feed bill."[9]

The sparring work lead to a four-round fight at Hollywood Legion Stadium. There he met movie star George Raft at ringside. Raft was a regular and an investor in the career of Henry Armstrong. Pep won his fight and a purse of $50. But the manager who arranged the bout kept $35 leaving our young lad with a measly $15. The boys decided to go home. They sold the car, borrowed $5 from the manager who stiffed them and took a bus back to New York.

Pep would later fight Ortiz after he became the featherweight champ. In pre-fight publicity Ortiz's manager (the same fellow from years before) said, "We paid him a dollar a round in California and he isn't worth much more than that. We won't have any trouble with him."[10] Pep won seven out of 10 rounds and earned $20,000. This an especially sweet payday considering what had transpired.

Majoring in truancy
Pep admitted that he was an ordinary student. "I didn't like school much and I liked it even less when I started

fighting amateur in my junior year."[11] Although he "kind of majored in truancy,"[12] he may have finished four years of high school (there is some dispute). Pep liked other sports, but, at only 105 pounds, his options were limited. He played shortstop on the baseball team where he graded himself as "good field, no hit."[13]

High school and job
Pep quit Hartford High School when he was 16. He worked for the Hoffman Wallpaper Company and got $13 a week as a stock boy. In two years he was making $20 a week, but then he turned pro and starting winning and making money as a boxer. Goodbye, Hoffman Wallpaper.

A winning amateur, a winning pro
Pep said, "I boxed 65 amateur fights. I was very successful in my amateur career. I won 62 of them. I boxed amateur about two and a half years, then I turned professional. I won fifteen or twenty in a row, and finally I didn't have to worry about going to work anymore. I made boxing my business. I won the featherweight championship of New England in March of 1942 and I won the championship of the world in November of that same year. I won 62 in a row. I won the championship of the world in my fifty-sixth straight win."[14]

Going pro, teaming with Bill Gore
Pep defeated Joey Marcus in his first professional fight in Hartford July 25, 1940. The winning did not stop until March 19, 1943 when he lost in a disputed (well, maybe in some minds) decision to Sammy Angott. Up to that point he had won 62 bouts in a row.

But I beat him

About the Angott loss Pep said, "He was lightweight champion of the world. I beat him. I didn't get it. That's all. I beat him in Madison Square Garden. They gave him the decision. I didn't have a mark on my face after the fight. I out-boxed him."[15]

And along came Gore

Bill Gore, who owned a gym in Miami, moved north and took over as trainer in early 1942. Gore saw the diamond in the rough. "One glance told Gore that Willie knew everything about the fine science of modified murder, but he had to be built up physically to improve his punch and stamina."[16]

Pep said, "I've got to give a lot of credit to my trainer, Bill Gore, who was pretty good for me. He was strictly a boxer's trainer, and me being a boxer, he fitted right in with me. I had the speed to burn, but I didn't know how to use it. Bill showed me how to use the speed, how to box. This is very important to have a good trainer like that."[17]

Getting the title shot in 1942

Pep buzzsawed through the division and the boxing world took note of the fighter with the "Golden-Boy Touch."[18] Among his victories included decisions over top-ten contenders Pedro Hernandez and Bobby "Poison" Ivy in August and September 1942, respectively.

Pep said, "I boxed everyone that was around. I boxed Bobby (Poison) Ivy, a local boy from Hartford, who was a pretty damn good fighter. I boxed Pedro Hernandez, who was number one challenger. That's how I got the

"I had the speed to burn, but I didn't know how to use it. Bill [Gore] showed me how to use the speed, how to box. This is very important to have a good trainer like that."

shot with Chalky Wright. I was matched with Chalky Wright, November 20, 1942, and I won a 15-round decision and the championship of the world."[19]

On top of the world

It would be difficult to overstate the qualifications and popularity of young Willie Pep in November of 1942 when he met Chalky Wright for the New York version of the featherweight championship. (There was some dispute as to who was the featherweight titleholder, but not very much — most considered Wright the king feather and Pep the number one contender.)

There had never been a winner like Pep. Victorious in 62 of 65 amateur bouts, he won the Connecticut State Amateur Flyweight Championship in 1938 and the Bantamweight Championship in 1939. As a young pro he had 53 straight wins, no losses. In March 1942 he defeated Johnny Compo to become the New England Featherweight Champion.

After the first Chalky Wright fight, it was reported in the February 27, 1943 issue of *Collier's* that Pep's winning ways were indeed historic:

It would be diffi-cult to overstate the qualifications and popularity of young Willie Pep in November of 1942 when he met Chalky Wright ...

Nate Fleischer, chief custodian of the archives of boxing, has checked back through more than two centuries and he reports that Willie's streak of fifty-six consecutive bouts without a draw or defeat (as of the end of 1942) is absolutely unprecedented in any era or weight division. Our Willie never has been in the remotest danger of being held even in a professional passage at arms. Taking a round from him is a stirring moral victory for the other guy.[20]

And the fans loved the boyish, boxer extraordinaire — especially those from his home state. After all, they saw most of his fights and saw him blossom as an amateur and pro. It looked as though most of Connecticut came down to New York to see him take it to the California boy, Chalky Wright. The fight would attract the largest crowd and generate the richest gate in indoor featherweight history.

The same *Collier's* article describes Pep's attraction:

For an understanding of Willie's extensive popularity in his home state, note must be made of an aberration peculiar only to Hartford and the surrounding countryside. Most localities are interested only in heavyweights, the muscular meatballs who can knock the other guy dead with a punch, but Connecticut is crazy about featherweights.

The Pep kid's recent ascension to the throne will nurture it for two more decades. Most small-town fight promoters are very happy indeed to average gross receipts of $1,500 for a show. In five fights at Hartford last summer, Willie drew $70,000 worth of clients.

The promoters, well aware that the people come to see Willie box, have been forced to change their programs. Instead of going on in the fifth bout at 10 pm, the feature spot for the headliner, Willie's fight always is the third event, at 9:15 pm, to permit the war workers on the night shift to report for duty at eleven o'clock.

The clinching demonstration of Willie's crowd-pleasing style came on November 20th of last year, the night he lifted Wright's title. Prior to that fight, Willie had appeared at Madison Square Garden in less than nine rounds, all in preliminaries. But the championship match established an all-time indoor feather-weight record for attendance and receipts. A thumping crowd of 19,521 paid $71,868 to see Willie's coronation.[21]

Chalky Wright

Wright was 30 when he fought Pep November 20, 1942. He was a very good fighter whose career began well, but slumped after the first five years. After another five years of mediocrity (and maybe a bit of fun with Mae West) he had enough luck left to be discovered by Henry Armstrong and his management team who guided him to the featherweight title in 1941. He could box and he could hit, scoring 81 KOs along with his 158-43-18 record. Wright was highly respected at the time and would become a Hall of Famer.

The *Boxing Register* has this to say about his run-ins with Pep:

The fact that he was unable to defeat Hall of Famer Willie Pep should not detract from Wright's accomplishments. He took on all comers, including lightweights and welterweights. He pos-sesses a fine left hook and a strong right. He could box on the outside or mix it up in close.[22]

Willie Pep, in his interview for *"In This Corner ..."* remembered that, "He was the hardest puncher that the featherweight division had had in the past twenty or thirty years. He could get you out with one punch. All he had to do was get you in the chin with one punch and he'd knock you out. He boxed welterweights. He was such a tremendous puncher they'd put him in with anybody."[23]

But it was just too late in the game for Wright to deal with a rising Willie Pep.

Champion of the world

There was great anticipation for this championship battle. Folks wanted to see a great fight and a great victory for a brilliant and popular young fighter. Pep was a 5-9 favorite. It was to be the biggest featherweight bout since Tony Canzoneri fought Benny Bass in 1928, 14 years earlier.

The fight was billed as a match between a soaring young star versus an ageless boxing sage — youth versus experience. Here's an expert from *The New York Times* on the day of the fight:

A free-swinging, hard-punching youngster from Hartford will seek to take the championship of his division from a ring-wise, crafty veteran at Madison Square Garden tonight. Willie Pep, pride of the Nutmeg State by virtue of his fifty-three consecutive triumphs in the professional ranks, will try to knock the featherweight crown from the brow of the ageless Chalky Wright in a fifteen-round clash, and so great is the interest in Pep's quest that a crowd of 17,000 fans is expected to watch the joust.[24]

An image shows a boyish Pep in gloves as large as his head dwarfed between manager Louis Viscusi and trainer Bill Gore.

The fight was billed as a match between a soaring young star versus an ageless boxing sage — youth versus experience.

The fight was in fact a showcase for the supreme defensive and counter-punching skills that Pep had accrued under the tutelage of trainer Bill Gore, and the valiant, yet plodding attempts by Chalky Wright to catch the prodigy and nail him with a knockout punch. Wright was able to land in the middle rounds, but could not put the boy away. He won only four rounds of the 15-round bout.

The following blow-by-blow review of the fight by *The New York Times's* James P. Dawson is a showcase in itself for the kind of exciting you-are-there boxing reportage that doesn't exist these days. Who needs film?

No other verdict was possible. Pep won off by himself by any basis of comparison. He captured eleven of the fifteen rounds in a defensive boxing display that saw him take the initiative infrequently.

Wright won four rounds — the fifth, sixth, seventh and eighth when he sailed in like a champion bent on destroying the lad who questioned his leadership.

Wright's fighting dictated this overwhelming vote. Aside from the four blazing rounds he won, the defending champion engaged in delayed-action manoeuvres that promised much and produced little.

Like a true champion, he pressed forward ceaselessly. Even when buffeted about on the end of Pep's long left jabs, Wright tore in, padded fists cocked, eyes alert, ready to let fly when the opening came. But the target never stood still, which is a commendation of Pep's vitality.

The fight was in fact a showcase for the supreme defensive and counterpunching skills that Pep had accrued under the tutelage of trainer Bill Gore ...

Wright had to hold his fire through most of the battle to avoid appearing ludicrous as Pep stuck and stabbed and broke and ran, piling up boxing points to an accumulation that only a knockout could erase.

In the late stages of the battle Pep was strong enough not only to be elusive but to turn at times and actually outslug the hard-hitting Wright in flurries which brought roars from the crowd that filled the Garden.

For almost five rounds Wright just plodded in, hardly unleashing a blow. However, he cut Pep's left eye in the fourth with a sweeping right. Wright cut loose in the fifth and almost keeled Pep over with a right to the jaw. He leaped in and whipped lefts and rights to the body and head. Pep was at sea. Near the end of the round Pep crossed two rights to the jaw and the crowd roared.

In the sixth, seventh and eighth Wright caught up with the retreating Pep and pummeled the Connecticut lad severely.

Pep seemed to take a new lease on life with the ninth, and
nicked Wright with several rights to the jaw when he wasn't
blinding the champion with stabbing lefts. In the tenth Wright
made one wild lunge after being sent off balance with a right
and left to the head, and almost toppled through the ropes.

Early in the eleventh, Wright hurt his foe with a terrific right, but
the rest of the session he pursued a boxing ghost. It was the
same right down to the finish because Pep kept stabbing his left
or pushing it to the face.[25]

An image shows Pep landing a sold left to Wright's head.
He appears considerably shorter than Wright (Pep was
in fact two inches shorter).

Tactics vs. Chalky Wright

Up to that point in time, Pep often pushed the fighting.
But instead of rushing in, he was ordered to dance and
retreat, use his left jab and never allow Wright to get set
to throw his right hand. Gore installed a sign in their
training quarters that said, "Don't Lose Your Head."[26] So
during the fight, Pep used the jab and made Wright miss.
He hated the strategy and in a later round asked Gore,
"Can I punch him now?"[27] Gore said if he deviated from
the plan, he would be crowned with the water bucket.

According to one observer, "It was not, frankly, a thrilling
fight, but it was an impressive exhibition of a twenty-
year-old boy's adaptability and intelligence."[28]

The part about not losing his head is very interesting
since it was certainly Pep's undoing in his brawls with
Sandy Saddler.

Pep said, "We trained hard for it. The idea was to stay on

Gore installed a sign in their training quarters that said, "Don't Lose Your Head." So during the fight Pep used the jab and made Wright miss.

the outside, hit and run, jab and run, don't stand still for the guy because if you stand still he'll get you out of there. This is what I did for 15 rounds. At the end of the eleventh, twelfth round I knew I was way ahead because he hadn't hit me. I was outboxing him. I make him miss quite a few punches, and this is the idea of the game: hit and not get hit. And that's exactly what happened. I made him look foolish, I guess, at times because he was missing me all over the ring, but this is the idea, not to get hit, and I won the championship."[29]

About that nickname

It was after a Chalky Wright fight (there were four in all) that Bill Corum of the *New York Journal-American* called Pep "Will o' the Wisp"[30] because of his elusive style (in his book, *Friday's Heros*, Pep said, "Maybe it should have been "Will o' the Wop."[31]) Although the nickname was applied to others including Abe Attell,[32] it's Pep who came to own it.

So he became the youngest featherweight champ since Terry McGovern. This was his 55th consecutive victory.

Pep would lose just once in his next 82 fights.

Sources for Chapter 3

Collier's

Fightbeat.com

Hartford Courant

Heller, Peter. *"In This Corner ...!": 42 World Champions Tell Their Stories.* New York, New York: Da Capo Press, 1994.

New York Times, November 20, 21, 1942.

Pep, Willie and Sacchi, Robert. *Friday's Heros.* Bloomington, Indiana: Author House, 2008.

Roberts, James B. and Skutt, Alexander G. *The Boxing Register.* Ithaca, New York: McBooks Press, Inc., 2011.

Sports Illustrated

Sugar, Bert Randolph. *Boxing's Greatest Fighters.* Guilford, Connecticut: The Lyons Press, 2006.

Footnotes for Chapter 3

1 Matt Eagan, "Ring Master: The Champ still has his corner," *Hartford Courant,* December 31, 1999.
2 Ibid.
3 Ibid.
4 Stanley Frank, "Fine Feather," *Collier's*, February 27, 1943.
5 Jim Shea, "Make Believe A Cop is Chasing You," Sports Illustrated, July 7, 1942.
6 Willie Pep and Robert Sacchi, *Friday's Heros* (Bloomington: Author House), 164-165.
7 Peter Heller, *"In This Corner ...!": 42 World Champions Tell Their Stories* (New York: Da Capo Press), 251.
8 Willie Pep and Robert Sacchi, *Friday's Heros* (Bloomington: Author House), 7.
9 Ibid., 8.
10 Ibid., 9.
11 Ibid., 99.
12 Ibid.
13 Ibid.
14 Peter Heller, *"In This Corner ...!": 42 World Champions Tell Their Stories* (New York: Da Capo Press), 251.
15 Kirk Lang, "From The Vaults — Interview with Willie Pep," Fightbeat.com.
16 Stanley Frank, "Fine Feather," *Collier's*, February 27, 1943.
17 Peter Heller, *"In This Corner ...!": 42 World Champions Tell Their Stories* (New York: Da Capo Press), 252.
18 Stanley Frank, "Fine Feather," *Collier's*, February 27, 1943.
19 Peter Heller, *"In This Corner ...!": 42 World Champions Tell Their Stories* (New York: Da Capo Press), 251.
20 Stanley Frank, "Fine Feather," *Collier's*, February 27, 1943.

21 Ibid.
22 James B. Roberts and Alexander G. Skutt, *The Boxing Register* (Ithaca: McBooks Press, Inc., 2011), 793.
23 Peter Heller, *"In This Corner ...!": 42 World Champions Tell Their Stories* New York: Da Capo Press), 251.
24 *The New York Times*, November 20, 1942.
25 Ibid.
26 Stanley Frank, "Fine Feather," *Collier's*, February 27, 1943.
27 Ibid.
28 Ibid.
29 Peter Heller, *"In This Corner ...!": 42 World Champions Tell Their Stories* (New York: Da Capo Press), 252.
30 Jim Shea, "Make Believe A Cop is Chasing You," *Sports Illustrated*, July 7, 1942.
31 Willie Pep and Robert Sacchi, *Friday's Heros* (Bloomington: Author House), 96.
32 Bert Randolph Sugar, *Boxing's Greatest Fighters* (Gilford: The Lyons Press, 2006), 136-137.

4. Early Saddler

It is no overstatement to say that the New York City Police Athletic League (PAL) was instrumental in Saddler's development as a boxer.

From Nevis to Harlem

Alexander Saddler, the "very tall"[1] father of Sandy Saddler, was born on the island of Nevis, British West Indies. A descendant of African slaves brought to work on English plantations, perhaps he was named for the island's most illustrious son, Alexander Hamilton, one of America's founding fathers, first secretary of the Treasury and early anti-slavery advocate.

Like his namesake, he made his way to Boston along with about 100,000 other West Indians who migrated to the United States between 1900 and 1924. There he married an American women, and a son, Joseph (who would later be known as Sandy), was born June 25, 1926.

When the boy was 2 or 3 they moved to Harlem, New York and took their place among a colony of West Indians (some 40,000 had already established a cultural base in the city, particularly in Harlem and Brooklyn). New York would remain home for the Saddler family and to at least one celebrity descendant, another Joseph Saddler, who became Grandmaster Flash, the pioneering hip hop artist and DJ.

Saddler's terrific amateur career scared the competition and vaulted him to the next level.

Besides Joseph, the family included three more boys and three girls. One sister, Judy, left a lasting impression on young Joseph. She was responsible for the two gold inlays that flashed each time he grinned. In a "playful moment"[2] while he was trying to nibble some cranberries off a countertop, she pushed his head into the marble (rough household).

Although he was "keen on basketball," he fell into boxing. "I liked boxing. When I was a kid I always did like boxing." He had a routine. "I went to school and at three o'clock I went to PAL to train and box."[3]

PAL helps save inner city kids — shapes the great fighter to be

It is no overstatement to say that the New York City Police Athletic League (PAL) was instrumental in Saddler's development as a boxer. PAL took the boy in, trained him and provided an opportunity to prove himself as an amateur athlete. Through his association with PAL, Saddler became a "solid and successful fighter"[4] under the tutelage of trainer Dick Bruno.

Fighting as a flyweight and bantamweight, he won 50 bouts and lost only three. By the time he was 17, Saddler couldn't get a match — no one would fight him (a reoccurring problem when he fought professionally). So he turned pro just shy of 18 years.

PAL

The Police Athletic League (PAL) began as a social movement in 1914. New York City Police Commissioner Arthur Woods set aside vacant lots and entire city blocks throughout the metropolis where children could play safely. By 1924 there were more than 100 blocks in the so-called Playstreets Project.

In 1931 the Twilight Baseball League was created which morphed into the Twilight Athletic League to include basketball and football programs. In 1932 this morphed into the Junior Police Athletic League which added boxing to the menu.

President Franklin Roosevelt lent his heft to PAL by allowing Work Projects Administration (WPA) workers to help staff the programs. By 1937 PAL had more than 70,000 junior members and operated 69 indoor centers. PAL was featured at the World's Fair in 1939 during PAL Day which included boxing demonstrations.

Although WWII curtailed PAL activity and threatened to shut it down entirely, public outcry led to refunding and continuity. PAL held a benefit at Madison Square Garden that featured movie stars and other celebrities including Rita Hayworth.

PAL is alive and well (and nationwide) today. The following is taken from their website:

PAL's mission remains unchanged — to keep young people out of trouble by channeling their energies into recreational and athletic programs. For more than 90 years, PAL programs have expanded to meet the new challenges faced by inner-city youth.

Source for this article
Police Athletic League, "History,"
http://www.palnyc.org/800-PAL-4KIDS/History.aspx

Introducing the young slugger

Saddler's terrific amateur career scared the competition and vaulted him to the next level. He'd say, "... I couldn't get any more fights. A lot of times they'd say 'All right, Sandy, we have someone for you.' I'd go out this night and they'd say the man didn't show up or something. I went back the following night, then went back the next week. There was no fights so I said let me go and turn professional and I went and turned professional in 1944."[5]

About that name

His real name was Joseph Saddler. A boxing publicist got the idea to turn him into a Scotsman, hence the nick-name Sandy. Photos were taken of him grinning in gloves and Scottish garb that included tartan (plaid) shorts and a tam-'o-shanter (a brimless cap with a bobble in the center).

He went on to wear plaid robe and shorts (sometimes) and was described as "... death in red plaid trunks"[6] by Philip Levine, working class poet and fight fan.

Hall of Fame management

Saddler deeply impressed boxing manager Charlie Johnston during an amateur show and took the boy banger on. Thus began a pro run for the ages.

Charlie was the younger brother of Jimmy Johnston (dubbed "The Boy Bandit of Broadway" by famed sports writer Damon Runyon) who had piloted the careers of Mike McTigue, Pete Latzo, Harry Greb, Ted Kid Lewis and Johnny Dundee — champions all. Dundee was the "Scotch Wop" who owned the featherweight title for so

The influence of Moore, who trained with the younger Saddler, was pivotal in Saddler's development and success.

many years. Jimmy also played a role in helping Jim Driscoll (another Hall of Fame feather) and Owen Moran win world titles.

But Charlie did OK on his own without big brother. Besides Saddler, Charlie managed Archie Moore, all-time knockout artist and light heavyweight champ. The influence of Moore, who trained with the younger Saddler, was pivotal in Saddler's development and success. (Saddler and Moore would go on to help coach and advise George Foreman during his first assent to the heavyweight title.)

What's up Jock
Saddler's first and second professional fights are noteworthy and somewhat intriguing. The first bout was set up March 7, 1944 with the help of Willie Pep's manager, Lou Viscusi. Bill Johnston (yet another Johnston — brother of Jimmy and Charlie) asked Viscusi to find a suitable first fight for Saddler and got Earl Roys, the New England champ.

It was a successful match-up for the Saddler camp as Saddler defeated Roys in an eight-round decision. At ringside were Pep and Viscusi who apparently enjoyed the evening with no sense of foreboding.

It made a second-tier fighter immortal because he's the only fighter who ever knocked Saddler out.

There was to be a return match two weeks later, but at the last minute Roys bowed out and was replaced with a more dangerous foe, Jock Leslie. Leslie was a solid fighter from Flint, Michigan who owned a successful amateur career before becoming a contender as a pro. He won the Michigan State Golden Gloves Championship as a bantamweight and later fought for the featherweight championship against Willie Pep in 1947, losing by knockout in the 12th round. His pro record was a respectable 58-14-4, with 14 victories by KO.

But no one bothered to tell Saddler about the change.

"I'm on a train going to fight Roys, as I think, and I see this fighter Jock Leslie that I've heard about, ask him what he's doing and he says he's going to Hartford to fight someone called Saddler. I said: 'No you ain't, cos that's me and I'm fighting Earl.' But Leslie was right, I found out soon enough."[7]

Leslie was too much for the kid at the time. Saddler would say, "I was TKO'd but I never was knocked out. He stopped me in about the third or the fourth round. He was much too experienced for me. He didn't knock me out or anything but the referee stopped the fight and said I couldn't continue because this guy was very clever."[8]

So the ups and downs of Saddler's first pro fights have Willie Pep's fingerprints all over them. Saddler's nemesis-to-be set the first fight up, which led (inadvertently) to his first and only KO defeat. Pep witnessed at least the first fight, and both bouts were held in Pep's hometown of Hartford, Connecticut. By the way, Pep fought and defeated Saddler's second opponent, Jock Leslie, in a championship bout three years later.

Saddler would talk about this unique defeat ruefully, "And ol' Willie's manager just thought he was doing me a favor ..."[9]

The defeat has grown in significance over the decades since it heralds the rise of an epic boxing career. Every bio of Sandy Saddler opens with his KO defeat at the hands of Jock Leslie — *every doggone one*. And there is a reason. It made a second-tier fighter immortal because he's the only fighter who ever knocked Saddler out. From then on Saddler pretty much had his way with most every opponent up to and including the mighty Willie Pep — who helped start the wheel turning in the first place.

"Phenomenal string of knockouts"
The Saddler camp was undeterred by the Leslie defeat. Mike Casey in his article "Sandy Saddler and The Long Road To Acceptance," says "... there was no period of recuperation or re-assessment. He was plying his trade in what was arguably boxing's most competitive era, when young prospects looking to get a foothold on the ladder simply couldn't afford the luxury of long layoffs and self-analysis."[10]

Saddler finished 1944 with a record of 19-2-1. That was 22 fights in his first pro year starting in March. He began his career as a bantamweight (116-118), but soon moved up to featherweight (123-126) where he gained most of his pugilistic glory. It should be noted that he also fought quite a few lightweight boxers (131-135) over the years.

In 1945, his second year pro, he fought 24 times and won 'em all. He had 17 KOs. Fourteen were consecutive. Seven came in the first round. The kid was usually knocking out an opponent every 14 days. (Wow!) And he still had to wait until October 29, 1948 for his title shot.

In 1946 he was ranked seventh best feather contender in the annual rankings by *The Ring* magazine (which makes you wonder what the other six guys brought to the table).

Pro record up to first Pep fight

The Boxing Register, ultimate source for boxing facts and figures, says in the Saddler bio, "With his phenomenal string of knockouts, Saddler probably deserved a title shot long before Pep finally agreed to fight him."[11]

And that's probably a big understatement. Indeed, Saddler's credentials for gaining a shot at Pep and the title were remarkable:

● Ninety-three fights, 85 wins, 6 loses, 2 draws, 56 KOs — over about four years.

● Thirteen fights in foreign countries, defeating seven national champions.

In 1945, his second year pro, he fought 24 times and won 'em all. He had 17 KOs. Fourteen were consecutive. Seven came in the first round. The kid was usually knocking out an opponent every 14 days.

● KO'd future lightweight champ Joe Brown in New Orleans in three rounds on May 2, 1947.

● Drew with future lightweight champ Jimmy Carter in Washington DC on June 3, 1947.

● KO'd his last three opponents — in three rounds or less — before the first bout with Pep on October 29, 1948.

"He had to fight me"

In an interview[12] from *"In This Corner ..."* by Peter Heller, Sandy Saddler describes the journey to the first battle with Willie Pep. After each selected quote, I chime in with a correction or explanation.

I used to fight maybe twice a week. I was knocking them off like two, three rounds. Back in the days when I was boxing, they had guys that were pretty good fighters.

The record shows Saddler averaged about two fights a month over the four years or so (94 bouts including the first Pep divided by 55 months), although there were plenty of bouts with only a few days between (no wonder he would remember those fights).

My sixty-sixth fight or sixty-seventh fight, that's when I actually

Interesting to note that he remembers there were 66 or 67 fights that led to the [title] bout when in fact there were 93 ...

fought for the title ... but today a guy have sixteen fights and there he is! He's a title contender already. Mainly, it's this: We haven't got any clubs going in New York. You have about two clubs in the area, but then you had about thirteen clubs ...

Interesting to note that he remembers there were 66 or 67 fights that led to the bout when in fact there were 93 (so many fights, easy to miss just 26). He mentions the lack of boxing clubs that negatively impacted the early training of aspiring fighters — not enough places or events for young boxers to learn. A problem that grew midcentury and is still with us.

I knocked out Joe Brown. Then I fought Jimmy Carter [to a draw]. I fought Orlando Zulueta for the junior lightweight championship and I won ... the championship ... but I never put it on the line. I was busy fighting these heavier guys, anyway. I was weighing 129 and fighting these guys that weighed 136, 138 pounds. I couldn't get the featherweights so the majority of them was lightweights.

I was number one contender and [Pep] had to fight me. I boxed in Argentina, Venezuela, Chile, Uruguay, Paraguay, I boxed in Panama, I boxed in the Philippines, I boxed in Cuba, and he just had to fight me.

Here he talks about all the heavier fighters he met, due in part because so many feathers wouldn't take him on. His ferocious reputation was, of course, valid and is one reason he boxed so much outside the United States. Pep was more of a homebody. He traveled to Canada three times and Nassau once.

Sample Saddler news clippings 1945-1947

Saddler vs. Johnson
Sandy Saddler, 125, New York, knocked Lucky Johnson, 128 1/2, Philadelphia, cold with his first punch ... *The New York Times*, January 16, 1945.

Sandy Saddler, 125, New York, knocked Lucky Johnson, 128 1/2, Philadelphia, cold with his first punch ...

Saddler vs. La Salle
Joe (Sandy) Saddler, 128, east side, knocked out Ralph La Salle, 120, Puerto Rico in 44 seconds of the first in a scheduled six-rounder. *The New York Times*, April 9, 1946.

Saddler vs. Terranova
Former Featherweight Champion Phil Terranova of New York punched out a close ten-round decision over his fellow townsman, Sandy Saddler before 5,000 spectators at the University of Detroit Stadium tonight. The taller Saddler piled up points in the early rounds, especially on infighting, but Terranova rallied in the later stages to get the decision. Terranova at 129 1/2 had a 4 1/2-pound advantage. *The New York Times*, July 24, 1946.

State Boxing Commissioner John J. Hettche today impounded Harlem featherweight Sandy Saddler's purse and ordered his manager, Charley Johnston, to appear before the commission to explain his action at last night's Saddler-Phil Terranova match. Following the decision last night, which went to Terranova, Johnston rushed Referee Sam Hennessy and noisily denounced the verdict. *The New York Times*, July 25, 1946.

In the semi-final, slated for six rounds, Sandy Saddler, 131, Bronx, knocked out Lou Marquez, 135, Puerto Rico, in 1:37 of the second. *The New York Times*, December 27, 1946.

Saddler vs. Zavala

Sandy Saddler, Jamaica lightweight, will head the card at the St. Nicholas Arena tonight. He will oppose the durable Mexican, Humberto Zavala, in a clash listed for ten rounds. The Jamaica boxer, who has lost only one of his twenty-one pro engagements, has scored knock-outs in his last six fights and is favored to swat down his Mexican foe. *The New York Times,* January 27, 1947.

Sandy Saddler, East Side featherweight, gave a ten-pound weight advantage to Humberto Zavala of Mexico last night at the St. Nicholas Arena and knocked out the game little lightweight in the seventh round of their scheduled ten-round feature bout. Saddler outboxed and outpunched his rival throughout. *The New York Times,* January 28,1947.

Saddler vs. Lewis

Featherweights met in the ten-round feature bout in the St. Nicholas Arena last night. They were Charley (Cabey) Lewis of Brooklyn, 130, and Joe (Sandy) Saddler of Harlem, 128. Saddler was the winner largely on his aggressiveness, as he constantly backed Lewis around the ring. *The New York Times,* April 15, 1947.

Sources for Chapter 4

Boxing Monthly, boxing-monthly.co.uk

Daniel Cann, danielcann.com

East Side Boxing, eastsideboxing.com

Greater Flint Area Sports Hall of Fame, gfashof.org

Heller, Peter. *"In This Corner ...!": 42 World Champions Tell Their Stories* New York, New York. Da Capo Press, 1994.

International Boxing Hall of Fame, ihof.com

The New York Times

Police Athletic League, palnyc.org

Roberts, James B. and Skutt, Alexander G. *The Boxing Register*. Ithaca, New York: McBooks Press, Inc., 2011.

Washington Afro-American

Weston, Stanley and Farhood, Steven. *The Ring: Boxing The 20th Century*. New York: BDD Illustrated Books, 1993.

Footnotes for Chapter 4

1 Daniel Cann, "Sandy Saddler: Featherweight Giant," http://www.danielcann.com/index.php/boxing/sandy-saddler#.Uhd4e0Z3z8U
2 *Washington Afro-American,* October 2, 1951.
3 Peter Heller, *"In This Corner ...!": 42 World Champions Tell Their Stories* (New York: Da Capo Press), 290.
4 Daniel Cann, "Sandy Saddler: Featherweight Giant," http://www.danielcann.com/index.php/boxing/sandy-saddler#.Uhd4e0Z3z8U
5 Peter Heller, *"In This Corner ...!": 42 World Champions Tell Their Stories* (New York: Da Capo Press), 290.
6 Stanley Weston and Steven Farhood, *The Ring: Boxing The 20th Century* (New York: BDD Illustrated Books, 1993), 69.
7 Neil Allen, "A Very Special Kind of Fighter," http://www.boxing-monthly.co.uk/content/0111/one.htm
8 Peter Heller, *"In This Corner ...!": 42 World Champions Tell Their Stories* (New York: Da Capo Press), 291.
9 Neil Allen, "A Very Special Kind of Fighter," http://www.boxing-monthly.co.uk/content/0111/one.htm
10 Mike Casey, "Sandy Saddler and The Long Road To Acceptance," http://www.eastsideboxing.com/weblog/news.php?p=6024&more=1
11 James B. Roberts and Alexander G. Skutt, *The Boxing Register* (Ithaca: McBooks Press, Inc., 2011), 724.

12 Peter Heller, *"In This Corner ...!": 42 World Champions Tell Their Stories* (New York: Da Capo Press), 291.

The first Pep/Saddler fight was a big surprise. The most successful boxer in history was KO'd in the fourth round by the sticks-for-legs, unheralded challenger.

Original caption: End of Ring Reign for Featherweight King. Sandy Saddler hovers over featherweight champ, Willie Pep, dumped to canvas in the fourth and final frame of scheduled 15-rounder at the Garden. It was a smashing left to the jaw which transferred Pep's title to Sandy.

Date Photographed: October 29, 1948

WIllie Pep vs. Sandy Saddler

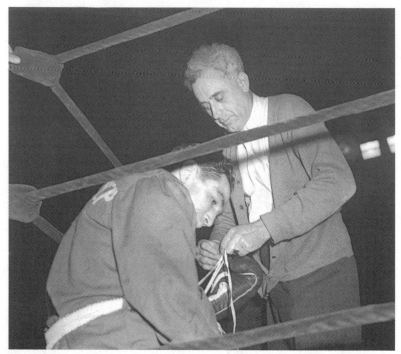

Pep was trainer Bill Gore's masterpiece. Gore taught him how to use his natural talents to become one of the immortals. Just as important was Gore's steady hand. Pep was a firecracker and needed the calming influence of the older man.

Undated photograph

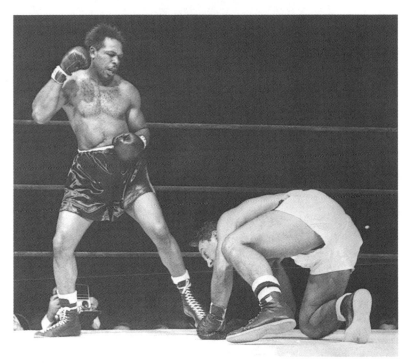

Archie Moore was the greatest knockout artist in boxing history.
He took the natural power and aggression of Saddler and
helped mold him into one of the great power punchers. Here
Moore has just knocked down the original Rocky — Rocky
Marciano.*

A shared trait between heavy and feather — Marciano had a reach of 70
inches, the same as Saddler — a remarkable physical characteristic for a 126
pound fighter.

Original caption: When the Rock Was Down. New York: Challenger Archie
Moore stands over heavyweight champ Rocky Marciano who was floored for a
count of four in the second round. It was the Rock's second time on the canvas
in his boxing career. Marciano came back to score a kayo of the challenger in
the ninth round.

WIllie Pep vs. Sandy Saddler

When Pep was on his game, he would make anybody look like a fool. Above, without throwing a punch, Pep used a spin move to send Saddler threw the ropes.

Original caption: Bronx, New York: This time it's Saddler's turn to hit the canvas, but it was only a slip.* Sandy said it was a kidney punch that really dethroned Hartford's Pep.

Date Photographed: September 8, 1950

*Not a slip. A review of the bout shows a spin and tumble.

The fourth bout was a street fight and is usually considered the dirtiest fight ever.

Original caption: New York: Wrong Sport? Featherweight champion Sandy Saddler (light trunks) and Willie Pep go tumbling over one another as they make like wrestlers in the title bout, Sept. 26, at the Polo Grounds. Referee Ray Miller, who stopped the fight in the eighth to warn Pep about wrestling, struggles to keep them apart and boxing in nearly every round. Saddler kept his crown when he was given a TKO in the 9th round.

Date Photographed: September 26, 1951

WIllie Pep vs. Sandy Saddler

Willie Pep (right) was a lively, likeable fellow. He was a hugely popular fighter and sought-after personality after he hung up the gloves.

Original caption: Two ring greats, ringers for each other, poke their head through the ropes at a boxing match in Miami Beach, Fla. The look-alikes are recently dethroned welterweight champs Carmen Basilio (left) and former featherweight titleholder Willie Pep. Their punch flattened noses probably account for the strong resemblance.

Date Photographed: April 6, 1956

Saddler knew how to grin, but he was never glib. Although he complained bitterly about his lack of regard from the boxing community, he had his day in the limelight as champion.

Original caption: Today one of the important events at City Hall was the opening of the 1949 fund raising campaign for P.A.L. (Police Athletic League). Present at the ceremony are (standing) L-R police commissioner Arthur Wallander; Sandy Saddler; Karl Drews, St. Louis Browns; Hank Majeski, Philadelphia Athletics; Bobby Thomson, New York Giants; George Stirnweiss, New York Yankees, and Deputy Commissioner James B. Nolan, President of P.A.L. Mayor William O'Dwyer is getting his P.A.L. card from Sandy Saddler, featherweight boxing champ. Goal of the drive is $1,000,000.

Date Photographed: January 25, 1949

WIllie Pep vs. Sandy Saddler

Saddler was relentless in the ring — the definition of bad intentions.

Original caption: Cornered in the 2nd. New York: Challenger Willie Pep buckles under the terrific pounding from the gloves of featherweight champ Sandy Saddler in the 2nd round of their scheduled 15-round title go at the Polo Grounds, September 26th. Pulling Sandy away is referee Ray Miller, who counted eight before Pep came to his feet. The ref stopped the bout in the 9th awarding the victory to Saddler, who kept his crown by scoring a technical knockout.

Date Photographed: September 26, 1951

Pep was all movement. A master of angles, his hand speed and footwork could make opponents look ridiculous.

Original caption: Willie Pep flattens his glove in the face of Fabela Chavez during the sixth round of their featherweight bout in St. Louis. Pep took a unanimous decision in the ten-rounder.

Date Photographed: November 19, 1952

WIllie Pep vs. Sandy Saddler

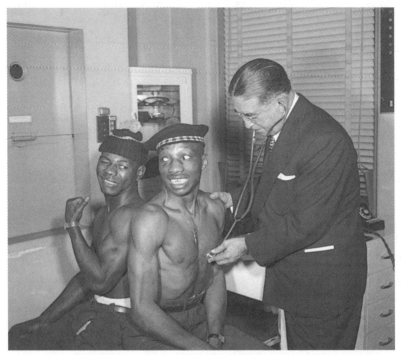

Sometimes Saddler just didn't look comfortable with his promotional duties. It didn't help that his ring persona was Scottish, hence the name Sandy, the tartan robe and the Tam o' Shanter. I never found a good reason, or any reason for this moronic ploy.

Original caption: Saddler and Davis Report for Pre-Title Fight Examinations. New York: Sandy Saddler, world featherweight champion, is examined by Dr. Nardiello at the boxing commission office, under the watchful eye of Red Top Davis, No. 1 contender for Saddler's crown. They meet at Madison Square Garden on Friday in a title bout.

Date Photographed: February 21, 1955

Pep, on the other hand, took to the promotional side like a fish in water. He loved to talk it up and the press loved him for it. His ring moniker — Pep — was absolutely correct.

Undated photograph

WIllie Pep vs. Sandy Saddler

In his prime, Pep was as good a boxer that ever lived. No one disputes that. Even when he was over the hill, some of that greatness flashed.

Original caption: Willie Pep, former featherweight champ from Hartford, Conn., lands a left [actually, a right] to the jaw of Andy Arel of Messena, N.Y., during the ninth round of their bout at Miami Beach auditorium. Although the 33-year-old Pep was badly cut about the face in the ninth, he won a unanimous 10-round decision over Arel.

Date Photographed: December 29, 1955

Saddler had it all. His 70-inch reach meant he dominated at range, but it was in close that he took them down with uppercuts and hooks. Note the musculature — lean and hard.

Original caption: Sandy on Target. New York: Featherweight King Sandy Saddler (left) lands with a left on the midriff of challenger Teddy "Red Top" Davis in the second round of their scheduled 15-round title bout.

Date Photographed: February 25, 1955

WIllie Pep vs. Sandy Saddler

Pep make it look easy. And he usually looked so good doing it.

Original caption: Almost. Famechon heads for canvas in sixth after absorbing some of Pep's lefts and rights, but ropes kept Ray from going all the way and he quickly gained an even keel.

Date Photographed: March 16, 1949

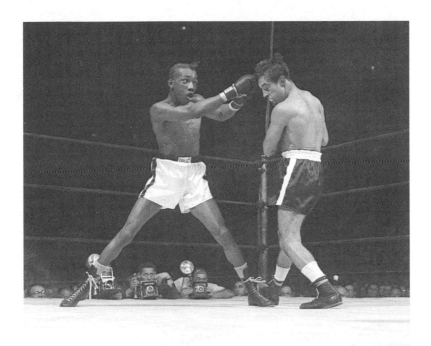

Saddler was not always pretty to watch. Tall, thin, all arms and legs — he didn't look like anybody's idea of a champ. The thing is, he took them apart anyway.

Original caption: Stab. Not content with just jabbing with his left, Saddler, (left) shoots both hands to Demarco's head in Garden struggle last night. Sandy won by TKO when Paddy was unable to answer the bell for the 10th round.

Date Photographed: October 28, 1949

WIllie Pep vs. Sandy Saddler

5. Pep pro

These were glory days — six years of fame, fortune and near invincibility.

The making of a legend

After winning the title, Pep lost just once in his next 82 fights before he was KO'd by Sandy Saddler on October 29, 1948. Of those, 24 fights were with a top 10 contender and six were title fights.

Solid boxers he beat over that six-year span included former National Boxing Association (NBA) featherweight champ Jackie Wilson (twice), NBA featherweight king Sal Bartolo (three times — his second victory on June 8, 1943 unified the world title because Bartolo was NBA featherweight champ at the time), current bantamweight champ Manuel Ortiz (in a nontitle fight), Chalky Wright (three more times including a KO) and former NBA featherweight champ Phil Terranova. He KO'd top contender Humberto Sierra in one of his two victories over him and defeated future lightweight champ Paddy De Marco.

These were glory days — six years of fame, fortune and near invincibility. "Pep danced in the spotlight, and the world cheered. He had drinks with Frank Sinatra, dined at Toots Shor's, wintered in Florida and beat everyone his handlers put in front of him."[1]

This is when he began to gain his legendary status. He was boxing's greatest winner. In 1945 he received the

"He turned boxing contests into ballets, performances by a virtuoso in which the opponent, trying to punch him out, became an unwilling partner in a dance, the details of which were so exquisite that they evoked joy, and sometimes even laughter."

The Ring magazine Medal of Merit as the outstanding boxer of 1945. Despite a near fatal plane crash and broken back in 1947, he recovered in five months to resume his winning ways. Arguably the best pound-for-pound fighter around, only Sugar Ray Robinson could begin to lay claim to that laurel.

Most (but not all) of the boxing press threw rose pedals and garlands.

Red Smith observed in the *Chicago Sun-Times*, "If Willie had chosen a life of crime, he could have been the most accomplished pick-pocket since the Artful Dodger."[2]

Members of the boxing press, "... were asking him where he had learned the marvelous moves which were second nature to him. He struggled to answer. It was like asking Hemingway where he learned to write."[3]

Jimmy Cannon, legendary sports journalist, wrote, "Sometimes there seemed to be music playing for him alone and he danced to his private orchestra and the ring became a ballroom."[4]

The great writer, W.C. Heinz, called Pep, "... the artist supreme." In his book *Once They Heard The Cheers*, Heinz wrote, "When I watched him box, it used to occur to me that, if I could just listen carefully enough, I would hear the music. He turned boxing contests into ballets, performances by a virtuoso in which the opponent, trying to punch him out, became an unwilling partner in a dance, the details of which were so exquisite that they evoked joy, and sometimes even laughter."[5]

There were naysayers. Some just didn't get his defensive style. The hit and run tactics may have piled on the points, but there was the idea that a champion should press ever forward. After defeating Chalky Wright for a second time on September 29, 1944, Joseph C. Nichols of the *New York Times* said, "Although he beat Wright, it is difficult to understand how he compiled so amazing a record on what he displayed last night."[6]

That one loss ...
On March 19, 1943 he finally lost a fight to former undefeated lightweight champion Sammy Angott (who would once again win the lightweight title.) But Pep said, "I beat him. I didn't get it. That's all. I beat him in Madison Square Garden. They gave him the decision. I didn't have a mark on my face after the fight. I out-boxed him."[7]

Writer Bob Considine described the bout as "a bar-room brawl — replete with ... slugging, rassling, and ... crushing football blocks."[8]

The story in the *The New York Times* the next day saw it as a solid win for Angott. It was reported that Pep waded into Angott's counters and could not overcome his early lead. Pep did in fact bloody Angott's face, but his damage came too late. He lost unanimously. It was a stinging loss considering his streak of wins, but a valuable lesson. Pep's best game was letting the other guy force the fight. Pep was a master at avoiding and countering any punch, then slipping away. He was much less effective mounting a straight-ahead attack, especially against a brainy foe.

Anomalies

It is telling and noteworthy that the loses of Pep (and Saddler) have earned so much attention over the years. That is because the loses were so few. Saddler was stopped (TKO'd) once in his career so Jock Leslie is always mentioned in a Saddler biography. Just like Sammy Angott is always noted as the guy who beat Pep, thus preventing him from having an undefeated record before his first fight with Saddler. Heck, Jimmy McAllister is usually noted for earning a draw with Pep over that period (Pep KO'd McAllister in two rounds in their second fight).

Time out for Uncle Sam

Pep served in the Navy and the Army. He was sworn into the Navy in June of 1943 and didn't fight again until April of 1944. Not such a long layoff considering what other fighters had to endure (Saddler was out all of 1953 during his Army stint).

Pep was sworn in June of 1943, made a troop leader and was quoted as saying, "I'll do my best. It's just like another fight."[9] But it proved to be a lousy experience for the champ as was a stint in the Army later on.

He certainly was not given special consideration. Pep said, "So I join the Navy and they made me water boy for the football team. I was champion of the world. Can you

"So I join the Navy and they made me water boy for the football team. I was champion of the world. Can you believe that?"

believe that? I hated the Navy. I was the water boy to the football team for Christ sakes. They treated me very unfair. I was in the Navy for two-and-a-half years." [10]

Oddly enough, he was inducted into the Army after leaving the Navy. "I was an MP in the guard-house. I did nothing to speak of. They gave me a gun and a club, and I used to go to sleep in the jailhouse. I was very poorly handled. I didn't get to give any speeches. Nothing." [11]

"I'm the only guy that won a round without throwing a punch"

Willie Pep often said that his greatest achievement was winning a round without throwing a punch. He carried around a news clipping that said as much and was always eager to show it. That alleged achievement is mentioned in many if not most biographies of the great boxer.

In an interview with *fightbeat.com* he was asked what he would want people to remember about him. He said, "That I was a pretty good fighter and that I'm the only guy that won a round without throwing a punch. I did it against Jackie Graves. I told a sportswriter before the fight I wasn't going to throw a punch. I spun him. I slipped punches. I blocked punches, but I didn't throw a punch. He fell down. He went through the ropes, but

> *"I told a sportswriter before the fight I wasn't going to throw a punch. I spun him. I slipped punches. I blocked punches, but I didn't throw a punch."*

he never hit me. I never hit him. So at the end of the round, the judges gave me the round, in his hometown. I was very proud of that."[12]

Fact or fable?[13]

On July 26, 1943 Pep fought a local boy, Jackie Graves, in Minneapolis. The story goes that a St. Paul sports writer, Don Riley, visited Pep before the bout. Pep suggested that he could fight a punchless round and "fake well enough to fool the judges and the spectators." It was decided that he would perform the feat in the third round.

It was, in fact, a rousing fight. It was reported that Pep went down twice and Graves nine times. Pep won by TKO in the eighth. But none of the reports at the time mentioned a punchless third. More importantly, Riley didn't say anything at the time either.

In 1970 Pep was interviewed by Peter Heller and made one of the first references to the punchless third. Pep said, "I jabbed him a few times, but most of the round, I was bobbing and weaving and making him miss."[14] (It is supposed that Pep must have meant his jabs were feints.)

So why didn't Riley say what happened back in 1946?

He said, "I was busy writing and doing broadcasts. It just slipped my mind."

Years later Riley finally wrote, "It was an amazing display of defensive boxing skill so adroit, so cunning, so subtle that the roaring crowd did not notice Pep's tactics were completely without offense."

In 2003 *cyberboxingzone.com* threw cold water on the story. Minnesota writer Jake Wegner wrote a story about the Pep-Graves fight and unearthed the original ringside report filed by Joe Hennessy of the *St. Paul Pioneer Press*. In that article Hennessy said that in the third round, "A clicker couldn't count the blows. Pep punched Jack [Graves] into the ropes as the most even round of the evening ended."

Although this reputes the punchless round story, there are those who don't think much of Hennessy's reporting. Some say the punches just didn't land.

"Joe Hennessy was a beautiful guy, but if you weren't clued in, you wouldn't realize Pep's punches were all feints," Riley said.

Some say the boxing reporting of that era was sloppy in general and that Hennessy was a bit spotty because of drink.

Ron Schara, a columnist for the *Minneapolis Star Tribune*, said that Hennessy, "came from the old school where the quality of a story varied depending on the number of cocktails he'd had. Joe had his share of those."

But Wegner doesn't quite believe Don Riley. He said, "Riley gives a different version of the story every time he tells it. He gets testy if you push him."

Some say Pep and Riley cooked up the story.

Riley said, "Why would I make up a story? What would I have to gain?"

Riley believes the story got out in 1968. There was a reunion breakfast and Riley "reminded" Pep about the third round. The story grew legs and Red Smith, *The New York Times* columnist, wrote about it in 1975. This is probably the news clipping that Pep tore out and kept in his wallet.

But Wegner said, "You don't keep a story like that on the back burner for 25 years." He said he has discussed the story with those who saw the fight and say the tale is untrue. They told him that, "Pep was fighting in the third round, not hiding behind the referee."

Another take is that the punchless third happened, but not with Graves. Pep had two other fights in Minneapolis in 1946 and just maybe Riley and Pep got the feat and the fighter confused.

So what is the truth? There is no film of the fight. Only the words of those who fought or saw a fight so many, many years ago. The fact that the story is not only still around, but also held as true by so many is testament to Willie Pep's otherworldly boxing ability — if anybody could win a round without landing a punch it would be Mr. Pep.

The fact that the story is not only still around, but also held as true by so many is testament to Willie Pep's otherworldly boxing ability — if anybody could win a round without landing a punch it would be Mr. Pep.

"I give Willie Pep the benefit of the doubt," said boxing historian Bert Sugar. So, it appears, do a lot of boxing (and especially Pep) aficionados.

Pep and the Hormel Hammerer[15]

The Pep-Graves bout of July 26,1946 is noteworthy for Pep's punchless third, yes. But there was more. The actual event featured at least 10 knockdowns, resulted in a record breaking gate (for Minneapolis anyway) and was attended by Minnesotan celebrities including a future presidential candidate.

Ringsiders agreed that Graves was "outclassed from the start but fought back gallantly and hit Pep as often and harder than any of Pep's other 104 opponents." Graves hurt Pep and the left hand he hit him with in the second round. After the fight manager Len Kelly said that it may need a cast. The "thrilling never-to-be-forgotten sixth round" saw Graves knock Pep down although Graves himself "went up and down like a hotel elevator during an American Legion convention."

Pep was put in a body cast for five months. He took it off and sailed into sporting history by winning seven bouts in 66 days.

Pep won by a TKO in the eighth.

After the bout Pep said, "He's a tough kid … it was a tough fight. I hit him as hard and as often as I've ever hit anyone. Yes, he has the style to beat any featherweight in the business, including Phil Terranova."

Graves, nicknamed the Hormel Hammerer (he worked for Hormel, the meat company), said, "Now I know how a champion fights. There is nobody tougher than Pep. I hope he gives me another chance in the future."

The gate was the largest in the history of boxing in Minneapolis, grossing $39,254.40.

In the balcony seats were Jay Hormel (Chairman of the Board of the Geo. A. Hormel & Co.) and Minneapolis Mayor (and future United States Senator and Vice President of the United States) Hubert H. Humphrey.

It was a different world for traveling champions back then. Pep had trouble finding a place to work out before the fight. Originally planning to train in an outside park, rains forced Pep to look for gyms. His first choice was already booked for "lady's reducing day." He finally found room at the YMCA.

Phoenix

In January 1947, Pep was seriously injured in an airplane crash, and most felt it marked the end of his career. But he made a remarkable comeback several months later, and defended the title he still owned by knocking out Jock Leslie (the same Jock Leslie that TKO'd Mr. Saddler) that summer.

Although Willie Pep thought his punchless third round was his greatest achievement, it's a pretty safe bet that most everyone else thinks his recovery from that plane crash ranks a bit higher.

Pep was flying back to Hartford from Miami when his chartered flight crashed in a snowstorm near Carmel, New Jersey. Three died and 18 were injured. Pep said, "I woke up on my stomach. People were moaning and groaning. The plane was ripped to shreds. My back was killing me."[16] That's because he suffered two cracked vertebrae as well as a broken leg.

Pep was put in a body cast for five months. He took it off and sailed into sporting history by winning seven bouts in 66 days. On June 17 he defeated Victor Flores. On July 8 he KO'd Joey Fontana. On July 8 he defeated Leo LeBrun. On July 11 he KO'd Jean Barriere. On July 15 he defeated Paulie Jackson. On July 23 he defeated top 10 contender Humberto Sierra. On August 22 he TKO'd Jock Leslie in his first title bout since the crash.

Up to this point Willie Pep had been a terrific winner.

He had been considered a boxing marvel.

He had been a very popular boxing personality — quick with the joke and simpatico, a catch-me-if-you-can artiste with a dash of aw shucks.

Now, climbing into the ring after the horror of a fatal plane crash, decidedly victorious again and again, Pep's journey became legend, and he one of the immortals. Rising from the ashes and carrying a 134-1-1 record into the first Saddler fight are feats forever etched in stone and account for his everlasting rank among the greatest.

"But I had my trunks."

According to Pep in his book, *Friday's Heros*, the New Jersey doctors couldn't determine the depth of his injuries. He transferred to a Hartford hospital where they discovered the broken vertebrae. Pep said, "If it had gone undetected much longer it would have healed wrong and I would have been a hunchback. It was my youth and my luck that got me over it."[17]

Pep wanted to begin training in June as soon as the cast came off. The doctors said he could walk in the park come October. Pep said no way, and after decasting, went straight to the gym. He told his manager to get him a fight.

Pep said, "five weeks later I had a fight. I'll never forget it, with a tough little Puerto Rican kid. Victor Flores, his name was. I went ten tough rounds. Now this was really a test because usually you get a guy you can easily handle, but this guy was there punching at me for ten tough rounds. There were two doctors at ringside and they were totally surprised. Those ten rounds with a tough Puerto Rican kid got me back on my way.

Rising from the ashes and carrying a 134-1-1 record up to the first Saddler fight are feats forever etched in stone and account for his everlasting rank among the greatest.

"I boxed a few more times and that September ... I defended my title against Jock Leslie, who was the number one contender, in his hometown. Now when you go into a hometown you've got to beat your man without a doubt or you won't get it, and this was for the Championship of the World. There was no problem as to who won the fight; I stopped him in eleven rounds.

"My loss was that the insurance company that I was suing, they said I was better than ever, so I didn't get any money from the plane crash. I think I got $15,000 for my expenses and after I paid everybody I was left with about $3000. I had sued for $250,000 but after I started boxing and winning the suit was thrown out. But I had my trunks."[18]

"And I was on my way"

The million dollar question was put to Pep in the *fight-beat.com* interview, albeit softly. Perhaps the interviewer should have phrased his questions more forcefully. Did the injuries affect his fighting ability? Was he the same boxer after the crash? Pep skips over the heavier implications and does not use his broken back as an excuse.

fightbeat.com: You broke your back in the 1947 plane crash you were in. Do you think you were a step slower when you returned to the ring?

Pep: "It has to slow you down, but I was always a speedster. They told me I'd never fight again but I said, 'Look, I'm a fighter.' I got hurt in January. I had a cast on my chest and a cast on my leg for five months. They took the cast off in June. I boxed in July. He was a tough kid. He kept coming but I kept out-boxing him, and I was on my way."[19]

... when he used his head and his speed, Pep was at his best and could easily out-point anybody, and he did for years.

Evolution, hints of what would be

Analysis of a few of Pep's fights shows an evolution and hints of things to come in the Saddler showdowns. In general, when Pep let the opponent come to him, his quicker feet and hands allowed him to counter and score, and in a few cases, KO his man. When he pressed without caution or let a brawler brawl or brawled back in return, he had more trouble.

Less careful in early fights, Pep could explode in the ring and become a whirlwind punching machine. He would overwhelm most, but he did lose once because of his thoughtless aggression. He had his problems with sluggers who could not box or opponents willing to rough it up. But if he refrained from brawling back and fought his fight plan, there was no stopping him. In other words, when he used his head and his speed, Pep was at his best and could easily outpoint anybody, and he did for years. The losing, especially in the Saddler fights, came when he underestimated his man and gave into temptations to brawl. A smart (and young) Willie Pep was unbeatable.

Sample Pep news clippings 1943-1948

Pep vs. Stoltz 1-29-43
Pep defeats Allie Stoltz in nontitle bout
No other decision was possible. Stolz won only one session, the eighth. For the rest, Pep simply overwhelmed his rival. The Hartford gladiator, a miniature Billy Conn with his wide-open style, reckless abandon in action, the speed of his flailing fists and his agility, swarmed all over Stolz at every turn. Pep hammered him from pillar to post ... *The New York Times*, January 1, 1943.

Pep vs. Angott 3-19-43
Sammy Angott defeats Pep in nontitle bout
Pep, winner of all sixty-two of his previous professional engagements, was soundly defeated by his veteran opponent, whose skill, awkward to the eye but effective in its application, enabled him to earn the unanimous verdict over his youthful rival.

Angott, who holds the post of boxing coach at Washington and Jefferson University, treated his opponent like a willing student in the first five rounds, then coasted the last five.

Angott boxed carefully at the start and forced Pep to come to him, landing sharp lefts to the head as Willie approached. Willie was willing, but his fire was inaccurate, and he rarely reached the "coach" with an effective punch. *The New York Times*, March 20, 1943.

Pep vs. Sal Bartolo 4-9-43
Pep defeats Sal Bartolo in nontitle, overweight bout
Bartolo forced the going most of the way, and it was his willingness to carry the action that cost him the verdict. For in his

eagerness he frequently was wild with his leads, and the alert Pep was quick to capitalize on these openings by flashing volleys of damaging left hooks to the head. *The New York Times*, April 10, 1943.

Pep vs. Bartolo 6-8-43
Pep defeats Sal Bartolo in featherweight title fight

... Pep was completely in charge. He forced Bartolo to make the first move almost every time and when this happened he would draw himself out of the orbit of Sal's punches and return a left-hand fire to the head that shook the local boy repeatedly.

Pep showed vast improvement. He delivered his left jab with sharpness and precision and actually outgeneraled Bartolo, whose forte was supposed to be his boxing ability.

Bartolo was wrestled to the canvas, coming out of a clinch in the thirteenth. *The New York Times*, June 9, 1943.

Pep vs. Wright 9-29-44
Pep defeats Chalky Wright in featherweight title fight

Pep, a 2-7 favorite, did little leading, forcing Wright to come to him in such a manner as to spray the challenger steadily with his left to the face. Wright tried to make a fight of it, but Willie knew exactly what he wanted to do and proceeded to do it. Round after round, as Chalky advanced, the champion merely stuck his left out, tapped Wright's face, then bounded out of harm.

When it came to infighting, Pep would have none of it. Whenever Wright took the action into close quarters, the champion caught him in a bulldog grip, and held until Referee Frank Fullam pried him off.

... Chalky, standing flat-footed, landed the harder punches, but his trouble was that he landed so few compared with the countless lefts that Pep fired at his face. From the fourth through the seventh Wright threatened an upset. He caught Willie repeatedly with rights to the head, and Pep seemed unable to offer anything in return. In the eight, though, the Hartford entrant solved Chalky, and once more resorted to the long-range, jumping-jack type of battle that had earned him the third. He fought that way to the end.

It was Pep's seventy-ninth victory in eighty professional starts. Although he beat Wright, it is difficult to understand how he compiled so amazing a record on what he displayed last night. *The New York Times*, September 30, 1944 by Joseph C. Nichols.

Against Terranova, Pep was a finished boxer, a master ringman, a skillful, cool, calculating master of the art of hit and get away ...

Pep vs. Terranova 2-19-45
Pep defeats Phil Terranova in featherweight title fight
With a masterful exhibition, of which few thought him capable, Willie Pep, world featherweight champion, retained his title last night as he gave rough, rugged, eager and willing, but painfully inadequate Phil Terranova of the Bronx a boxing lesson in fifteen rapid rounds at Madison Square Garden before 10,247 fans. The receipts amounted to $48,701.

Boxing like a master, handling himself like anything or anyone but the ring clown to whom local boxing followers have become accustomed, Pep galloped impressively to his eighty-sixth ring triumph in a career of eight-seven bouts, carrying off a unanimous decision over the stout-hearted little Bronxite, to which none objected.

This Pep was a revelation last night. Heretofore he has been a slam-bang sort of a fighter, a veritable whirlwind in spasmodic flashes; a miniature, modified Harry Greb, throwing punches from all angles and indiscriminately as he charged a foe.

Against Terranova, Pep was a finished boxer, a master ringman,

[Pep] threw the weapon, sharply and forcibly, to the point of McAllister's chin, and Jimmy blinked.

a skillful, cool, calculating master of the art of hit and get away, in a demonstration of boxing science that was inescapable, the more so since it came so unexpectedly.

Of course, Terranova accentuated the beauty of Pep's performance. The Bronx lad, former champion of the National Boxing Association, is a slugger with no pretense at boxing skill. He will jab on occasion, but his forte is punching, and he relishes the going at close quarters.

Obviously fully aware of this, Pep saw to it that there was no close-quarter fighting. He made Terranova fight the champion's way and, though the action was comparatively unexciting early in the fray, the onlookers who appreciated boxing skill had the thrill of seeing in action a spindly legged little fighting man who outthought, outmaneuvered, outguessed his rival at practically every turn. *The New York Times*, February 20, 1945 by James P. Dawson.

Pep vs. McAllister 3-1-46
Pep KOs Jimmy McAllister in nontitle bout

Pep looked like a newcomer and McAllister like a skilled titleholder until hostilities reached their sudden end. For in the first round the Baltimore boy seemed to have things all his own way. He hooked and jabbed Willie with his left, and deftly stayed out of range of anything Pep threw at him. Things proceeded along these lines in the second too, until Pep delivered the two punches that turned the lights out for McAllister.

The latter's left had bothered Willie through the second, and Jimmy became overconfident when he found it so easy to hit his rival. So he tried to tag Willie with a long right to the head, and that's where he made his mistake. Willie drew himself out of range and when the blow had spent its force the Hartford fighter struck back with a right. He threw the weapon, sharply and forcibly, to the point of McAllister's chin, and Jimmy blinked.

There was some who thought that Pep would have trouble with McAllister because he had been held to a draw by the Baltimore fighter in the latter's home town three months ago. *The New York Times*, March 2, 1946.

Pep vs. Junior 7-28-48
Pep KOs Young Junior in nontitle bout

Pep knocked out Young Junior tonight in 2:45 of the first round of a nontitle bout. Junior ... sailed into Pep at the start with sharp rights to the body, but the champion countered with a series of jabs. A left hook to the jaw sent Junior reeling and a right to the jaw finished him. *The New York Times*, July 29, 1948.

Pep vs. DeMarco 9-10-48
Pep defeats Paddy De Marco in nontitle bout

Willie Pep beat Paddy DeMarco .. Pep had some trouble with his younger rival, but there was no doubt in the mind of anyone except De Marco as to who won. Balloting in Pep's favor was unanimous.

De Marco showed no end of willingness. He rushed at Willie constantly and threw punches from every angle. The greater part of his blows, though, were avoided. In close quarters De Marco mauled and tugged away repeatedly, seeking to hit Pep from any and all points.

Against these wild tactics Pep could do nothing except return in kind, with the result that there was a considerable amount of inside rough stuff that made for a lot of furious action but which hardly made for a show of skill. Pep's greater strength and "savvy" enabled him to come out of the struggle with the decision.

There were few rally hard blows struck ... each fighter was on the floor several times as the result of slips or shoves.

In the opening session De Marco rushed but Pep was cautious
and remained out of range. In the second, Paddy threw a football block at Willie and shoved him through the ropes. Willie
returned to punch his foe about the head with both hands.
The New York Times, September 11, 1948.

Lead into Saddler fight

At this point, following the lone loss to Angott, Pep was
on a streak of 73 fights without a loss. His record stood
at 134 wins, 1 loss, 1 draw.

Pep and his team had no fear going into the title fight
with Sandy Saddler in October 1948. Pep was at the
height of his stellar career. In practical terms, he had
beaten three fighters who beat Saddler: Jock Leslie, Phil
Terranova and Humberto Sierra. Pep called him "a thin,
weak-looking guy who looks like you could go 'poof' and
knock him over."[20]

But the risk was right there for anybody to see. A pre-
fight article in *The New York Times* on October 29, 1948
notes that the challenger had compiled 63 KOs in 93
professional fights. And that he defeated six Latin-
American champions on a long road to the title fight.

Nobody was going to blow Saddler away.

Reader please note: Numbers of wins, loses and draws under
the last subheading disagree with other sources. This is a
common enough occurrence as one digs into all the old clippings. But the reader should get the general idea.

Sources for Chapter 5

espn.com

fightbeat.com

The Guardian

Heller, Peter. *"In This Corner ...!":* *42 World Champions Tell Their Stories.* New York, New York: Da Capo Press, 1994.

The Milwaukee Journal

The New York Times

Pep, Willie and Sacchi, Robert. *Friday's Heros.* Bloomington, Indiana: Author House, 2008.

Roberts, James B. and Skutt, Alexander G. *The Boxing Register.* Ithaca, New York: McBooks Press, Inc., 2011.

Sports Illustrated

startribune.com

Sugar, Bert Randolph. *Boxing's Greatest Fighters.* Guilford, Connecticut: The Lyons Press, 2006.

thesweetscience.com

Footnotes for Chapter 5

1 Jim Shea, "Make Believe A Cop is Chasing You," *Sports Illustrated*, July 7, 1942.
2 Ibid.
3 Red Smith, *The Milwaukee Journal*, February 3, 1959, (From *NY Herald* copyright 1959).
4 Michael Carlson, "Willie Pep," December 1, 2006, http://www.guardian.co.uk/news/2006/dec/02/guardianobituaries.boxing
5 Pete Ehrmann, "Few Did It As Well As Willie Pep," November 23, 2006, http://www.thesweetscience.com/article-archive/2006/4684-few-did-it-as-well-as-willie-pep
6 *The New York Times*, September 30, 1944.
7 Kirk Lang, "From The Vaults — Interview with Willie Pep," Fightbeat.com.
8 Michael Carlson, "Willie Pep," December 1, 2006, http://www.guardian.co.uk/news/2006/dec/02/guardianobituaries.boxing
9 *The New York Times*, September 30, 1944.
10 Kirk Lang, "From The Vaults — Interview with Willie Pep," Fightbeat.com.
11 Ibid.
12 Ibid.

13 Most of the information under this subhead comes from the following source: Don Stradley, "Could Pep have won a round without landing a single punch?" August 6, 2008, http://sports.espn.go.com/sports/boxing/ news/story?id=3522638

14 Peter Heller, *"In This Corner ...!": 42 World Champions Tell Their Stories* (New York: Da Capo Press), 253.

15 Ben Welter, "Willie Pep and the Hormel Hammerer," November 25th, 2006, http://blogs2.startribune.com/blogs/oldnews/archives/130 (This is a posting of an article by Frank Diamond, *Minneapolis Tribune*, July 26. 1946.)

16 Jim Shea, "Make Believe A Cop is Chasing You," *Sports Illustrated*, July 7, 1942.

17 Willie Pep and Robert Sacchi, *Friday's Heros* (Bloomington: Author House), 12.

18 Ibid., 13.

19 Kirk Lang, "From The Vaults — Interview with Willie Pep," fightbeat.com.

20 Bert Randolph Sugar, *Boxing's Greatest Fighters* (Gilford: The Lyons Press, 2006), 8.

6. First fight

Pep walked into a wrecking ball on October 29, 1948. It wasn't even close.

And so it begins — the first fight

Pep walked into a wrecking ball October 29, 1948. It wasn't even close. He lost the first two rounds, got floored twice in the third and knocked out in the fourth.

The first round saw Saddler press the attack with body shots and hard left jabs. Pep returned fire and tried to bring the fighting inside, but was wrapped up by Saddler. After separating, Saddler resumed the attack to the body with left hooks. Pep's nose was bloodied.

Pep got in some shots in the second, but was peppered with Saddler's relentless left jab to the head.

In the third Saddler continued to press — Pep's punches having no effect — and punished Pep with both hands. Midway in the round Saddler knocked Pep down with a left hand. He got up at nine, was dealt a left hook and a right to the jaw and went down for another nine. The bell may have saved him.

The next round saw Saddler spring into a series of rights to the jaw. Pep's return was "feeble" and at 2:38 of the fourth was knocked out by a left hook.

It certainly can be argued that the fight was decided before the bell rang. The challenger trained with pent up purpose. The champion did not.

In summary, Joseph C. Nichols of *The New York Times* said Pep, "had little spring in his legs, no sharpness to his punching and an inability to get away from a tantalizing, and at the same time punishing, left to the face that Saddler constantly threw at him."[1] Pep let Saddler force the fight "without reck"[2] and the challenger "went about carving up Willie with sharp lefts to the face and short rights to the body and head."[3]

For the sophisticates reading this

On a side note regarding *The Times* article, Pep was referred to as "Willie" a number of times. Saddler was "Saddler" and never called by his first name. A lack of regard, perhaps. Pep inspired an affection that sometimes passed Saddler by.

Also the words! "Tantalizing" here means to torment, not so much to tempt or tease, which is how we have come to know the word. "Reck" — a word lost to most of us — means to pay heed.

Fix rumor nixed

The bout was rumored to be fixed, that Pep was to take a dive. The hint of foul play was enough for Chairman Eddie Eagan of the New York State Athletic Commission to address the fighters at the noon weigh-in the day of the bout. He said, "I am holding you responsible to uphold the good name of boxing. There are rumors of a 'fix' before every fight, but we don't pay any attention to them. You are two honest athletes fighting in a great class for a great championship. You will represent boxing tonight."[4]

Pep said, "Don't worry about me. I'll be there to win."[5]

Saddler, as was his wont, said nothing.

In his report, Nichols said, "the manner in which he [Saddler] disposed of Willie made it clear no collusion was necessary, that he had enough guns at his disposal to take care of Pep on his own. The battle simply proved that Willie didn't have enough to hold off the eager young Negro."[6]

After the bout, Chairman Eagan said, "Both boys did their utmost."[7] He was reported to say that there were easier ways to dump a fight than swallowing Saddler's savage punches for four rounds.[8]

The photo alongside *The New York Times* report of the fight shows Pep prostrate at the feet of Saddler. Two things must have jumped out at readers at the time. First, Pep down and out on the canvas (he'd never been KO'd professionally). And second, those long, skinny legs of Saddler looming over Hartford's favorite son. *Did the owner of those sticks really do all that damage?*

Preparation was key

It certainly can be argued that the fight was decided before the bell rang. The challenger trained with pent up purpose. The champion did not.

Saddler had been waiting in the wings with his evermore fearsome record for years and was ready to fight for the crown. In his corner was one of the famed Johnston brothers, Charlie, who knew something about coaching champion boxers. Saddler's real weapon, however, was the great Archie Moore who was also trained by Johnston and took a special interest in the young Saddler's title shot with Pep. Moore was another fighter who knew all about waiting for title shots — he finally got his at age 39 (or thereabouts since his birth date is disputed) when he pummeled Joey Maxim for the light heavyweight belt in 1952.

From Moore, Saddler learned how to slip, get inside, cover up properly and use his punching power. Saddler said in an interview with Peter Heller, "Archie taught me quite a bit how to punch, punching from the ball of my feet. That was very important."[9]

Moore sparred with Saddler and impressed upon him the need to press the fight. Saddler said in the same interview, "He wanted me to stay on top of him, give Pep no leverage, because if you gave Pep any leverage, for chrissake, you could clean forget it then."[10]

And forcing the action on an uncharacteristically hesitant Pep indeed won him the battle. "[I] stayed on him and as he relaxed I would punch. I just kept on like that until I actually knocked him out, knocked him stoned in

"I just kept on like that until I actually knocked him out, knocked him stoned in that fourth round. Out. You could count 50, pal, I'm telling you."

that fourth round. Out. You could count 50, pal, I'm telling you."[11]

Won't do that again
Pep made two big mistakes, and he readily owned both right away. First, he went into the fight with an arrogance only the greatest winner in boxing history (which he was at the time) would have. He said, "I was in good shape but he just overcome me. He got me cold and he knocked me down and they stopped the fight. I went down two or three times. I held him too lightly."[12]

And he went into the fight unprepared. He said, "I wasn't ready mentally for a tough fight."[13]

Pep made sure he was ready for the next one.

"Saddler then broke through with a left to the nose, and there was an audible crack as the blow landed and sent Beato down for the count."

Brief interlude

After the first and before the second bout
Pep/Saddler II came about three months later on February 11, 1949. Pep fought twice during that time and won two decisions. Saddler fought five non-title bouts and won them all with two KOs, two TKOs and one decision.

Saddler's work was particularly impressive.

Audible crack
About three weeks after the first fight with Pep, Saddler KO'd Tomas Beato in the second round. *The New York Times* reported that during an exchange, "Saddler then broke through with a left to the nose, and there was an audible crack as the blow landed and sent Beato down for the count."[14]

Short work
A few weeks later Saddler went to Cleveland and KO'd his man in the second. *The New York Times* said, "Saddler caught Giosa against the ropes and nailed him with a hard left hook to the kidney. The painful blow caused Giosa to drop his guard and Saddler then floored him with another left hook on the chin."[15]

Master at every turn

Less than two weeks later, Saddler TKO'd Terry Young, aka Angelo DeSanza, a top 10 contender. James P. Dawson of *The New York Times* said, "On his boxing and slugging, Saddler proved Young's master at every turn. Young, shorter in height and with a shorter reach than Saddler, rushed the champion for the first three rounds, seeking to get close, pound the body and reduce Saddler to size. The plan failed because Saddler proved himself even more effective than the slugging East Sider in the close-range, short-arm punching when he wasn't tilting Young's head back on the end of snappy left jabs."[16]

Lost his way

Angelo DeSanza came from a rough place, earned a good bit of success with his fists, but lost his way. He was sent to reform school at 16. In 1943 he began a two-and-a-half year term in Sing Sing after admitting he had led a gang in a series of hold ups. He fought more than 100 bouts including opponents such as Pep, Saddler and Beau Jack. He was considered for a title shot, but it fell through. He was shot to death in November 1967 at the 13th Street Playboy Social Club on the Lower East Side (Manhattan). He was 46 years old.[17]

Rough battle?

"Saddler knocked out Young Finnegan of Panama tonight in 2:52 of the fifth round ... The lanky sharp-shooting Saddler buried a left in Finnegan's midsection and then nailed a hard right to the jaw in the decisive round. The Panamanian collapsed in his own corner. Up to that point it was a rough battle."[18]

In the limelight: Saddler remembers PAL

In his first official act as champion, Saddler appeared at the opening the Police Athletic League's Fund Drive. As we have noted, Saddler learned how to box and competed as an amateur with the PAL boxing programs.

The New York Times article of January 17, 1949 reported that the 1949 campaign to raise one million dollars was opened by Mayor O'Dwyer at City Hall along with a group of professional athletes. Like Saddler, each had been a PAL participant.

The image over the article shows the mayor engaged with Saddler as the other athletes look on. They included the legend-to-be Bobby Thompson (who would hit the "Shot Heard Round the World," a game- and pennant-winning home run for the New York Giants against the Brooklyn Dodgers on Oct. 3, 1951), Hank Majeski of the Philadelphia Athletics and George Stirnweiss of the New York Yankees.

The article went on to say that the 1949 budget "will provide an athletic program for 300,000 boys and girls."[19]

Sources for Chapter 6

The New York Times

Heller, Peter. *"In This Corner ...!": 42 World Champions Tell Their Stories.* New York, New York: Da Capo Press, 1994.

Weston, Stanley and Farhood, Steven. *The Ring: Boxing The 20th Century.* New York: BDD Illustrated Books, 1993.

Footnotes for Chapter 6

1 *The New York Times*, October 30, 1948.
2 Ibid.
3 Ibid.
4 Ibid.
5 Ibid.
6 Ibid.
7 Ibid.
8 Stanley Weston and Steven Farhood, *The Ring: Boxing The 20th Century* (New York: BDD Illustrated Books, 1993), 83.
9 Peter Heller, *"In This Corner ...!": 42 World Champions Tell Their Stories* (New York: Da Capo Press), 292.
10 Ibid.
11 Ibid.
12 Ibid., 253.
13 Stanley Weston and Steven Farhood, *The Ring: Boxing The 20th Century* (New York: BDD Illustrated Books, 1993), 83.
14 *The New York Times*, November 20, 1948.
15 Ibid., December 8, 1948.
16 Ibid., December 18, 1948.
17 Ibid., November 6, 1967.
18 Ibid., January 17, 1949.
19 Ibid., January 26, 1949.

Willie Pep vs. Sandy Saddler

7. Second fight

The bout was Ring Magazine's Fight of the Year *in 1949 and is considered by many ring historians to be among the all-time classics.*

Fight of the year, fight of a career

Pep made the most of his return match with Saddler and then some. In a performance universally acclaimed as "wondrous,"[1] Pep fought the "fight of his life"[2] in a battle "savagely waged."[3] The victory made him the first feather to win back the crown after losing it. The bout was *The Ring Magazine's Fight of the Year* in 1949 and is considered by many ring historians to be among the all-time classics.

On February 11, 1949, only three months and 13 days after being leveled by Saddler, Pep fought him for a second time and won on all three cards by at least a three round margin.

Saddler was the favorite at 5 to 7 just before the fight. The odds fluctuated a bit during the day — Pep was the choice at 5 to 7 after the noon weigh-in. According to James P. Dawson of *The New York Times*, the consensus was that Saddler would win by a knockout.

But the reporter went on to say that Pep "is a fighter of windmill style, tireless and with resourcefulness and baffling speed. He is champion again today because he has

In the first, he landed 37 jabs successively "in a demonstration of blinding speed that had Sandy looking like a novice."

all these ring essentials, with unflagging courage as well."[4]

"Jumping in and out, twisting and turning, pushing and pulling,"[5] Pep was able to thwart Saddler's dangerous inside game and won seven of the first eight rounds. In the first, he landed 37 jabs successively "in a demonstration of blinding speed that had Sandy looking like a novice."[6] Pep continued to give Saddler a "boxing lesson"[7] through the first three rounds.

But Saddler did not make it easy. Pep was weakened in the fourth with body shots and a hard left jab. A right hand cut Pep's left eye in the fifth, but Pep ignored it and outboxed Saddler in this round and each round thereafter through the ninth. Dawson reported that, "In fitful bursts Pep hammered Saddler with lefts and rights from all angles and in tireless fashion, while Saddler missed most of his blows."[8]

Saddler did gain some traction as the fight wore on and landed a very hard right to the jaw in the tenth. This blow had Pep "teetering."[9] It was reported that Saddler's onslaught was so effective that ringsiders thought the fight would be stopped.

But Pep once again rallied and "electrified"[10] the crowd with his acumen through the 11th, 12th and 13th rounds. Dawson wrote that Pep, "pelted Saddler with every blow known to boxing."[11]

The fourteenth saw a stronger Saddler rock Pep with a right and left hook to the jaw which "shook the Hartford gladiator to his toes."[12]

But Pep answered the call in the fifteenth and final round. Dawson said, "He came back to fight Saddler all over the ring with a strength that few, if any, thought he possessed."[13]

At the final bell Pep was exhausted — "doubled over and desperately hanging on to Saddler's waist."[14] With blood streaming from his damaged face, Pep did not look like the winner. Afterwards he took three stitches over each eye, three on his left cheek and two on his right.

"I don't think he'll fight me again,"[15] said Sandy Saddler, perhaps alluding to the damage he'd done. But the boys were only halfway through their rivalry — there was still more history to make.

"I cut him up and whatnot"
In his interview with Peter Heller, Saddler showed a grudging respect for Pep's great night. Not dismissive or belittling in any way, he still manages to understate what the rest of the boxing world saw as a fistic feat for the ages.

"One of them things. He put on a very good boxing exhibition. He pulled and he slipped and he carried on. He fought a very good fight and he beat me a 15-round decision. I stayed on top of him and I cut him up and whatnot but he just got that decision over me."[16]

"I realized how great it was to be champion"

Pep, as usual, was more expansive. It wasn't just his greatest fight, it was Saddler's as well! It's easy to see that it was a very important win for him — to come back like that after such a devastating loss. The boxing world found one more reason to love this fighter Pep.

Three months later I won it back. The greatest fight of his life and the greatest fight of my life. Sandy's a good, quick fighter. I make up my mind to get in better shape and not hold him lightly. He was full of confidence. He had knocked me out. He had all the confidence oozing. I had to overcome that and I did in a 15-round fight. It was a very, very tough fight. I had to keep on the go. He hit me some pretty good punches, he shook me up a few times. All I know is I was on my toes for 15 rounds and I knew I was in a fight. I out boxed him and win back the title. That was the greatest night of my life. I realized how great it was to be champion again. And I know I won it from a good fighter.[17]

Hints of what would be

In shades of things to come, Pep was warned for wrestling in the first round and for heeling (raking the face with the laces of a glove) in the third. After the fight Saddler's manager, Charlie Johnston, protested the actions of Referee Eddie Joseph to the New York State Athletic Commission (NYSAC).

According to *The New York Times* report released two days after the fight, Johnston said, "everything the referee did was advantageous to Pep and damaging to Saddler."[18] He said the ref let Pep get away with heeling, spinning, hitting from behind, wrestling, stepping on feet and pushing.

"I knew I was in a fight. I out boxed him and win back the title. That was the greatest night of my life. I realized how great it was to be champion again."

He also said the ref would not let the fighters engage in infighting, Saddler's greatest strength. He claimed Joseph held Saddler's arm when he made his frequent breaks, thus mitigating Saddler's offense.

In reply, Referee Joseph said there was no serious violation of boxing rules. He knew, however, that the fight would be a rough one because Saddler refused to shake hands with Pep before the first bell.

He went on to say that, "There was a little roughness, but none of it was too bad. Saddler would grab Pep around the waist and punch the kidneys, holding and hitting. Pep stepped on Saddler's toes and pushed him off balance.

"I cautioned Pep for heeling in the third round. Before the round started I ordered Pep's handlers to remove some vaseline they applied to Pep's left arm and neck, obviously to prevent Saddler's locking the arm in close or getting a firm grip on Pep's neck in the close-range fighting."[19]

He had this to say about the infighting or lack of it: "I tried to keep the fighting at long range, out in the open,

He knew ... that the fight would be a rough one because Saddler refused to shake hands with Pep before the first bell.

so that the action would be clean; to keep the boys from getting too rough at close quarters ..."[20]

The New York Times reported on February 26 that Chairman Edward P.F. Eagan of the NYSAC dismissed criticism of the bout. The article pointed out that Johnston did not seek a reversal of the decision. Johnston requested Chairman Eagan to insist upon a third meeting between Pep and Saddler. Eagan said he would unhesitatingly approve such a bout if a promoter presented contracts.

So what was all the huffing and puffing about? Perhaps Johnston was lobbying for a less intrusive referee for the next fight. After all, a very big part of Saddler's attack was his inside game, featuring left hooks, short rights and devastating uppercuts. And maybe a few dirty tricks.

Did the lobbying pay off? There certainly was a return fight. And, of course, another after that. Each bout had a different referee — Ruby Goldstein refereed the third fight, Ray Miller the fourth. And it can be said — without a doubt — that neither of the last two fights suffered from too much officiating.

Nuggets
Pep weighed 126, Saddler 124. The smaller man still the most powerful.

On the cards, Pep really dominated this one. The judges had it 10-5, 9-5-1, 9-6 for Pep. *The New York Times* (Dawson) had it 12-3.

The fight set a new indoor record for a featherweight championship bout — 19,097 fans paid $87,563 to break the previous record of $71,869 for the Pep vs. Wright match of 1942. It was reported that 5,000 fans were turned away. Promoters were dreaming of an outside venue that would attract a gate worth $250,000.

Some split

Saddler's take for the first fight with Pep was 10 percent of net receipts. Pep received 50 percent. *The New York Times* article reported that they each got 30 percent for the second battle, "a concession that drew commendation for Saddler."[21]

Perhaps we should remember this grand gesture when we judge this man.

Lull, sort of

There was a lull between storms after the second Pep vs. Saddler of about 18 months. That is, a lull between those two. The boys kept very busy knocking off just about anybody who wanted to climb into the ring with them.

Pep had 15 fights, three of which were title defenses — all wins including two KOs and one TKO.

Saddler had 23 fights and won them all. Only five went the distance. The record shows 10 KOs and eight TKOs. One of his victories, his bout with Orlando Zulueta, earned him the vacant world junior lightweight title (127-130). He would defend this belt twice in as many years.

Then there was nobody else to fight but the other guy.

Pep honored by home state

Four days after his victory, Pep got the star treatment in his hometown of Hartford, Connecticut. Governor Chester Bowles gave him a silver trophy and the state legislature passed a resolution calling Pep "the greatest champion of them all."[22] It further stated that Pep's "matchless achievement" in regaining his title "has written a bright new chapter in the history of boxing."

Let's get married

Pep's winning ways were pretty much trumped by his no-show for a July 10 bout with Bobby Bell in Washington in order to get married and go on a honeymoon. His manager, Lou Viscusi, received a telegram that simply said, "Getting married today. See you in a week.

"He [Pep] didn't appear until the morning of the fight — and with a bride he had acquired the evening before. But that time the fight went on."

Willie."[23] Apparently Pep got his dates mixed up.

Pep drew a suspension from the National Boxing Association (NBA) for his lapse.

But it was just more of the same for the guy putting on the fight, Goldie Ahearn. *The New York Times* reported that, "Pep ... executed a similar matrimonial play ... about eight years ago. He didn't appear until the morning of the fight — and with a bride he had acquired the evening before. But that time the fight went on."[24]

Pep was 27, his bride 22. It was the second marriage for both. Pep would have four more to go. His six marriages are consistent with the Willie Pep Saga — lotsa wins, losta laughs, losta stories and losta wives.

Ultimate showdown
The stage was set for the third and biggest fight.

Pep was the comeback kid. Surviving a plane crash and a broken back, he had come back to defend his title and resume his winning ways. Then Saddler happened. Underestimated and overwhelming, Saddler demolished this "paragon of perfection"[25] and suddenly Pep looked like yesterday's news. But Pep came back again and fought his greatest fight, took back the crown and won

"Pep will pit his magnificent boxing skill against the tallest feather-weight extant. Moreover Saddler is one of the hardest hitters the division ever has known."

the adulation of Boxing Nation.

Saddler was the Knockout King — rough and ready. He had toiled for years to get his shot and shocked the fistic world by taking out the brilliant Pep. But the second bout saw him unable to catch the dancer. He usually missed with his powerful strikes, and as a result, looked foolish. But he didn't miss all the time. He tore Pep apart and finished almost unmarked. He lost on points, not damage done.

It would be the largest crowd and the biggest gate for a featherweight title bout since Johnny Dundee defeated Eugene Criqui of France at the Polo Grounds on July 26, 1923.

The venue was Yankee Stadium, no less. The Governor of Connecticut was coming. The New Haven Railroad announced a "Willie Pep Special" that would carry 600 fans from Hartford and points surrounding.

Saddler was the favored fighter, but James P. Dawson of *The New York Times* suggested otherwise: "The outcome depends on the physical condition of Pep. If it's as good as last time, he should win."[26]

Dawson said, "Pep will pit his magnificent boxing skill against the tallest featherweight extant. Moreover Saddler is one of the hardest hitters the division ever has known."[27]

Expectations were high. It was going to be a great fight.

Sources for Chapter 7

The New York Times

Heller, Peter. *"In This Corner ...!": 42 World Champions Tell Their Stories.* New York, New York: Da Capo Press, 1994.

Sugar, Bert Randolph. *Boxing's Greatest Fighters.* Guilford, Connecticut: The Lyons Press, 2006.

Weston, Stanley and Farhood, Steven. *The Ring: Boxing The 20th Century.* New York: BDD Illustrated Books, 1993.

Footnotes for Chapter 7

1 Stanley Weston and Steven Farhood, *The Ring: Boxing The 20th Century* (New York: BDD Illustrated Books, 1993), 84.
2 Bert Randolph Sugar, *Boxing's Greatest Fighters* (Gilford: The Lyons Press, 2006), 8.
3 James P. Dawson, *The New York Times*, February 12, 1948.
4 Ibid.
5 Stanley Weston and Steven Farhood, *The Ring: Boxing The 20th Century* (New York: BDD Illustrated Books, 1993), 83.
6 James P. Dawson, *The New York Times*, February 12, 1948.
7 Ibid.
8 Ibid.
9 Ibid.
10 Ibid.
11 Ibid.
12 Ibid.
13 Ibid.
14 Stanley Weston and Steven Farhood, *The Ring: Boxing The 20th Century* (New York: BDD Illustrated Books, 1993), 84.
15 Ibid.
16 Peter Heller, *"In This Corner ...!": 42 World Champions Tell Their Stories* (New York: Da Capo Press), 292.
17 Ibid., 253-254.
18 *The New York Times*, February 13, 1949.
19 Ibid.
20 Ibid.
21 Ibid., January 5, 1949.
22 Ibid., February 16, 1949.
23 Ibid., July 11, 1950.
24 Ibid.
25 Arthur Daley, *The New York Times,* September 8, 1950.
26 James P. Dawson, *The New York Times*, September 8, 1950.
27 Ibid.

8. Third fight

What promised to be great became chaotic and a thing beneath what these two men could create in a bout with each other.

Roar and crash

The third battle roared through seven rounds ... and crashed. Pep owned the night up to the abrupt, unsatisfying finish and "amazed most with a characteristic battle in which he out-thought, out-maneuvered, out-boxed, and, at times, out-fought the dashing, crashing Saddler."[1] But like the second fight there was "uncertainty about the veteran Pep's ability to avoid and/or withstand the battering blows of the heavier hitting Saddler."[2] Indeed, Saddler found his mark on occasion and in the third knocked Pep down.

Unfortunately the most significant factor in this fight (and the last) was the specter of a fight out of control. What promised to be great became chaotic and a thing beneath what these two men could create in a bout with each other.

Rounds one and two

Pep took control of the fight from the get go — his boxing mastery apparent and extraordinarily effective. Saddler was once again the pressing threat, but unable to score against "One of the most difficult targets the ring has ever known."[3] Pep "jabbed Saddler dizzy,"[4] landed left hooks to the body and rights to the head. He had Saddler "all at sea."[5]

Pep "jabbed Saddler dizzy," landed left hooks to the body and rights to the head. He had Saddler "all at sea."

Round three

Saddler came alive in the third. He charged through Pep's offense and connected with a left hook to Pep's jaw that sent him to the canvas. Unhurt, Pep took a nine count and suffered a "blazing volley"[6] that left a cut under the left eye and a bloody nose. Pep countered with left jabs and hooks and an occasional right. Saddler came away with a knot under his left eye.

Round four

Saddler charged hard looking for the KO. Another hook grazed Pep's jaw, but this only signalled another "furious"[7] counterattack by Pep. The latter outjabbing and even outpunching Saddler as he deftly avoided one powerful strike after another.

Round five

Pep was in control, no doubt about that. It was in this round that one of the more noteworthy events of the rivalry occurred. Pep ducked a Saddler hook, retreated to the ropes, took Saddler's elbow, gave it slight twist and sent Saddler flying.

In the film that has survived, Pep is seen casually rearranging his trunks as Saddler sprawls. In a photograph of this action, Saddler is hurtling in midair as if shot from a cannon. The slight of hand (looking a lot like a Judo move) is almost laughable. The little guy is making Saddler look silly. One can easily imagine how furious this made the tripped-up Saddler.

Round six
Saddler resumed his fruitless assault and got wilder as Pep's brilliant boxing peaked.

"Ducking under his foe's blows, cracking an overhand right to the face or head, or swinging a left to the body in combination with a right to the head, Pep had Saddler bewildered and helpless to stop or counter his fire."[8]

The rough stuff began in earnest when Saddler tried to wrestle Pep to the floor in a clinch.

Round seven
Pep carried on as before, but suffered a series of left hooks to the body that may have turned the fight. He "continued to pepper and stick and stab"[9] with his ubiquitous left jab and was ever accurate with punches to Saddler's head and body. At this point in the bout, Pep was leading on two of the cards. One judge had them even. *The New York Times* reporter Dawson had it six to one for Pep.

It was looking like a repeat of the second fight. Then the tussling got even uglier.

Salty
The editors of *Ring Magazine*, in their book *Boxing The 20th Century*, have a more egalitarian take on the fight. After the third round, the fighting "turned salty"[10] and both fighters roughed it up. This report says, "Pep

pushed, pulled, thumbed and stepped on Saddler's toes. Saddler wrestled and punched where he wasn't supposed to."[11]

At any rate, in the final seconds of the round, the boxers clinched in a neutral corner and in the ensuing push and tug Pep sustained a dislocated shoulder. Pep could not answer the bell for the eighth round and the fight was declared a TKO for Saddler.

Dull thud

The result was a complete failing of expectations. Fans were excited to see if the nimble champion could box his way around the hard hitting challenger. Would it be like the first fight — where Saddler overwhelmed, or the second — where Pep shined so bright? For almost seven rounds the fans got what they paid for, but the final result was a rotten apple. A dislocated shoulder? In a championship fight? Between these two guys?

James P. Dawson of the *The New York Times* said, "It was unfortunate the bout ended as it did. It finished abruptly a bout that was proceeding at a blazing pace between a marvelous little boxer and a slugger who was stalking his prey waiting for the kill he so confidently had predicted in advance; unfortunate, too for its effect on Pep's status. For, the defending champion undeniably was on the road to victory. The only question was whether he could maintain the terrific pace. Indications were that he could."[12]

Official word

The shoulder injury was no joke. Dr. Vincent A. Nardiello diagnosed the injury as a dislocated left shoulder and

"It finished abruptly a bout that was proceeding at a blazing pace between a marvelous little boxer and a slugger who was stalking his prey waiting for the kill he so confidently had predicted ..."

authorized the announcement Pep could not continue. Two other doctors checked him out and concurred. They were Drs. Alexander Schiff and Charles Muzzicato.

Pep complained of severe pain in his left shoulder and inability to move it in any direction. Examination in the ring by Dr. Nardiello showed he sustained a subluxation, a dislocation of the left shoulder, which was immediately "reduced"[13] by Dr. Nardiello. Examination in the dressing room also disclosed a soft tissue swelling and immediate X-ray had been ordered.

What they said

Pep complained bitterly. "He got a double-arm lock on me in that last clinch on the ropes in the seventh round, and that's what did it," said Pep. "I felt a crack in my shoulder and couldn't raise the arm when I went to my corner."[14]

No doubt referring to the body attack that preceded the clinch, Saddler said, "I thought a punch to the kidney did it. But if they say I twisted his arm, okay, I twisted it."[15] Interesting reply. Saddler didn't appear to care what any-

Saddler admitted to wrestling, saying "that's how Willie wanted it." He went on to say, "I know I had him in the third, but I was in no hurry."

body thought. As if saying: *I had him beat with my hands, but if you wanna say different, be my guest.*

This sort of casual menace is a reoccurring trait in Saddler's remarks to the press. Is it for real? It's a little hard to believe when you see the images of that wide, golden grin.

But it has been said that the young Saddler was ruthless. George Foreman, two-time heavyweight champ and grill king said, "As a boxer, Sandy was vicious. There is no other word to describe him in the ring. He would try to really put that into me. When he was in the ring, he knew nothing about retreat. Everything was about get him, get him, get him."[16]

"I was in no hurry"
The New York Times also reported that Pep said he was beaten by the grappling move. "I couldn't use my arms the way he did, but if I could I'd have won." He also indicated that the damage under his left eye was not done by a punch. Pep said, "He butted me here early in the fight."[17]

And again, Saddler admitted to wrestling, saying "that's how Willie wanted it." He went on to say, "I know I had him in the third, but I was in no hurry."[18]

The article reported that, "The ex-champion [Pep] was in considerable pain in his dressing room interview, and had to be eased by a sedative." But the clip goes on to say that he is "eager" for another fight with "his two-time conqueror." [19]

And so it came to pass.

Record gate
Fans numbering 38,781 turned out, paid receipts of $262,150.41, a record for a featherweight title contention.

On his butt
The image next to *The Times* article dated September 9, 1950 has Pep sitting on his fanny, elbows resting on knees, looking down and resting — waiting for Referee Ruby Goldstein to start the count (Pep would rise at nine). As he waits, Goldstein is shown walking Saddler to a neutral corner. Saddler is looking back at Pep. This was action from the third round.

Willie Pep vs. Sandy Saddler

Sources for Chapter 8

espn.com

The New York Times

Weston, Stanley and Farhood, Steven. *The Ring: Boxing The 20th Century.*
New York: BDD Illustrated Books, 1993.

Footnotes for Chapter 8

1 James P. Dawson, *The New York Times*, September 9, 1950.
2 Ibid.
3 Ibid.
4 Ibid.
5 Ibid.
6 Ibid
7 Ibid.
8 Ibid.
9 Ibid.
10 Ibid.
11 Ibid.
12 Ibid.
13 Ibid.
14 Stanley Weston and Steven Farhood, *The Ring: Boxing The 20th Century*
(New York: BDD Illustrated Books, 1993), 92.
15 Ibid.
16 George Foreman, *Saddler was vicious in ring*, October 11, 2001,
http://sports.espn.go.com/espn/classic/news/
story?page=foreman_on_saddler
17 *The New York Times*, September 9, 1950.
18 Ibid.
19 Ibid.

9. Fourth fight

Still a road warrior, Saddler had five fights outside the United States — in Cuba, Argentina (three bouts) and Chile.

Leading into the fourth fight

There was a little more than 12 months between the third and fourth battles. Both fighters kept busy. The Saddler camp very much so.

Pep fought eight times, winning them all — three TKOs, five decisions, no top 10 contenders.

Saddler fought 14 times. He lost decisions in nontitle bouts to two top 10 contenders, Del Flanagan and Paddy DeMarco.

His 12 wins included five KOs, three TKOs and four 10-round decisions. He defeated two top 10 contenders. One fight was a junior lightweight title bout with Diego Sosa in Havana in February 1951. He KO'd Sosa in two rounds. Still a road warrior, Saddler had five fights outside the United States — in Cuba, Argentina (three bouts) and Chile.

Here's sampling of Saddler fights. I found no NYT articles for Pep during this period! How soon they forgot.

The ideal Boxer versus the ideal Slugger showed up for maybe a minute or two for the first fight, perhaps most of the second, maybe six rounds of the third and maybe two rounds of the final.

Rampage

His KO of Sousa in Havana almost incited a riot. It was reported that "... police had to escort Saddler and the referee from the ring when the crowd of 10,000 yelled 'foul.' Cushions and bottles were thrown into the ring ..." (Foul for what was not stated.)[1]

Juan and Eva

He traveled to Buenos Aires and defeated lightweight Alfredo Prada in June, 1951. The bout drew 30,000 fans, including President Juan Peron and wife Evita. They all came "to see the first fight a world champion ever ... had in South America." Prada was KO'd in the fourth. Saddler "battered him from the start."[2]

De Marco a puzzle

Paddy De Marco upset Saddler later that August in a split decision in the second of their three matches (Saddler scored a ninth round TKO in their first fight in October, 1949). "De Marco started charging from the opening bell, pushing Saddler against the ropes with his arms and body to keep the champion from opening up at long ranges."[3] De Marco outweighed Saddler 136 pounds to 128 1/2.

Saddler would lose again to De Marco in December, 1951 in another split decision (that Saddler strongly disputed). The last bout was reported to be a stepping stone toward getting a crack at the lightweight title[4], thus especially disappointing to the Saddler tribe when De Marco triumphed.

Dark angels

The ideal dynamic that defined the war between Pep and Saddler was Boxer versus Puncher. The world of boxing contains both fighting styles, of course, and all fighters have a blend of both. And some are more boxer than puncher and vice versa. In the case of Pep and Saddler, one fighter was one of the greatest boxing artists of all time and the other one of the most dangerous sluggers (pound for pound). For those interested in the clash of these timeless styles, you would be hard pressed to find purer examples of each. That's what made the best parts of their bouts truly great and why we still celebrate these two men who made their marks in the middle of the last century.

But what is an ideal? It's perfection. It's an abstract. It's what could be. The ideal Boxer versus the ideal Slugger showed up for maybe a minute or two for the first fight, perhaps most of the second, maybe six rounds of the third and maybe two rounds of the final. We can be grateful for that I guess.

In the first fight the prepared Slugger demolished the unprepared Boxer. In the second, the Boxer's best met with the Slugger's best and history was made. In the third, good fighting gave way to something less than that. In the fourth fight there was chaos when both men ignored their wonderful talents and took their art to a very dark place.

It's amusing to watch the old film of that fight. So funny it could be a template for a comedy. One can almost see a favorite pair of actors thrashing it out on the screen like old Willie and Sandy did so long ago.

But in the end that's also why it's tragic. Both of these remarkable boxers turned away from what could have been and instead created something a great deal less. Something mediocre. The same guys who gave us one of the greatest fights of all time also gave us one of the worst. Hard to believe. But it happened and in writing about it right now I am still stunned. Something happened on their way to glory that September night in 1951.

Nat Fleisher

Fleisher was founder of *The Ring* magazine, aka the "Bible of Boxing." *The Ring*, founded in 1922, became "the authoritative voice on boxing" and established annual rankings of fighters. This magazine also chose fights and fighters of the year. Fleisher used the magazine to speak out on boxing issues and became a "moral voice" for boxing. He also published *Nat Fleisher's Ring Record Book and Boxing Encyclopedia* (from 1941-1987). *The Ring* is still going strong and remains a powerful institution in the boxing world.

Source
Roberts, James B. and Skutt, Alexander G. *The Boxing Register.* Ithaca, New York: McBooks Press, Inc., 2011.

Shakespeare, Dickens and Lincoln used the phrase "better angels" to describe a more noble aspect of humanity. Listening to our better angels means we are striving to do what is best — we are taking the high road. But that's not always easy. Passions can run amok and lead to chaos.

"Any resemblance to the accepted theory of boxing as a 'fair, stand-up' exhibition of skill between two perfectly trained, well-matched, sportsmanlike individuals was purely coincidental ..."

" ... the shadows of our own desires stand between us and our better angels, and thus their brightness is eclipsed."[5]

Highfalutin for a pair of prizefighters? How better to describe the worst parts of the Pep vs. Saddler rivalry?

Shadows prevailed for both fighters in this final fight. It was ugly and there was a lasting price to pay.

"A disgraceful brawl"

A somewhat modest crowd of 13,786 "witnessed a wild melee complete with heeling, gouging, tripping, butting, pushing, shoving, and wrestling. Nat Fleisher labeled the bout 'a disgraceful brawl.' "[6]

James P. Dawson of *The New York Times* reported "For roughness, disregard of ring rules and ethics, and wild fighting, this surpassed anything seen in the three previous meetings of these bitter ring rivals. Any resemblance to the accepted theory of boxing as a 'fair, stand-up' exhibition of skill between two perfectly trained, well-matched, sportsmanlike individuals was purely coincidental ..."[7]

" ... Referee Miller would have been justified in tossing both out of the ring."

"Good evening, gentleman"

It was reported that after Referee Ray Miller called Pep and Saddler to the center of the ring for instructions he said, "Good evening, gentlemen."[8] This courtesy was "something new"[9] and as things turned out supremely ironic.

The first two rounds had a familiar ring. Saddler connected a time or two, and when he did, caused damage. Pep, though, shook off the initial blows and at times dominated with his boxing. Once again, it was Pep the Tactician versus Saddler the Destroyer.

In round one, Saddler struck first with a hook to the jaw. But Pep provided a "boxing lesson"[10] with lefts and rights to the face and hooks to the body. Saddler was warned for holding and hitting.

Early in the second, a left hook cut the eyelid of Pep's right eye and this was the beginning of the end (the eye would get much, much worse as the fight progressed and ultimately lead to his undoing). Later, a body hook dropped Pep for an eight count. But he "rallied superbly"[11] before the bell and "rock[ed] Sandy with a big right ... pot-shotting him with thirteen unanswered blows."[12]

After round two the "roughness"[13] began in earnest and the bout spiraled out of control. The round by round report after the fourth reads like a street fight.

Saddler was "wrestled down"[14] in the fifth.

Both fighters fell to the canvas from "body holds"[15] in the sixth.

Pep was charged with "unnecessary roughness"[16] in the seventh. Referee Miller got tangled with the fighters while trying to separate them and went down in a chorus of laughter and jeers.

Saddler was wrestled down once more in the eighth and there ensued "a mild exhibition of strangling."[17]

At the end of the ninth round, "Pep was all in. Slumped forward on his stool, he seemed to be looking for someone or something to pump fresh oxygen into his lungs and fresh ambition into his heart." [18]

Confusion reigned when Pep remained seated. He told the ref he could not go on. "An unidentified second"[19] in Pep's corner tried to countermand the fighter's decision to quit, but was ignored by Miller who indicated the fight was over. He summoned Dr. Vincent A. Nardiello, state athletic commission physician, to examine Pep. Saddler's manager, Charley Johnston, got worked up and began arguing that something was amiss regarding the role of Nardiello. The crown rumbled and roared it's disappointment.

The New York Times reported that Pep complained that his right eye "was bothering him."[20] He was "found to be all right, though indisposed, and left the ring under his own power."[21] These were understatements.

The truth was that his eye was swollen shut and a horrible mess. Pep would say, "I couldn't see at all. You can't fight with one eye, not against Sandy Saddler, and not in a fight like that. It was over."[22]

Mike Casey describes the damage wrought to his face as "one of the all-time great shiners, an absolute peach of a black eye that would have stopped King Kong in his tracks."[23]

An image of Pep and his ruined eye is proof positive that a stoppage was in order. Although Pep made the call on his own behalf, his corner and/or the referee probably should have stepped in sooner. Most certainly such an injury would stop a fight today. As would all the fouls earlier. But as Pep would say in yet another understatement regarding this fight, "... the referee didn't do much."[24]

"These boys don't like each other."
Dawson of *The New York Times* said, "For a world championship battle it was a sorry spectacle. Both fighters were guilty of the collar-and-elbow, rough-and-tumble style of fighting made famous on the waterfront."[25]

Pep was ahead on the official cards when he "surrendered."[26] Referee Miller had it five rounds to four. Arthur Aidala had it four, four and one, but Pep ahead on points, 8 to 6. The other judge, Frank Forbes, had Saddler in front, five rounds to four. Dawson had it for Saddler, six rounds to three.

In the dressing room Pep was mad at everybody. He said,

"I couldn't see at all. You can't fight with one eye, not against Sandy Saddler, and not in a fight like that. It was over."

"I had to fight the other guy, the referee and City Hall."[27] City Hall?

Saddler said, "I figured to fight cleanly and started to do so, but Pep started it. He was heeling, thumbing, stepping on my toes and wrestling all night."[28] Saddler would stick to his blamelessness his whole life.

Dawson said, "... Referee Miller would have been justified in tossing both out of the ring."[29] If only he could have.

The new Chairman of the State Athletic Commission, Robert K. Christenberry, was at the fight and said, "these boys don't like each other."[30]

Christenberry would soon have much more to say. Among his first official acts was to investigate the fight. His commission collected reports from boxing officials and held an open hearing with both fighters in October.

Following the money

The fourth fight drew a much smaller gate. The interest in these two had waned considerably. Saddler continued to occupy a lower earning level despite his dominance. He earned a larger percentage for the fourth battle after his victory in the third, but the percentage was smaller than Pep's for the third after his victory in the second.

"You can't fight with one eye, not against Sandy Saddler, and not in a fight like that."

Go figure. The dollar amounts in parenthesis are 2012 dollars.*

Some 13,868 fans attended the fourth fight with gross receipts of $75,311 ($665,037 adjusted).[31]

Saddler received 37 1/2 percent of net proceeds and Pep 22 1/2 percent. The net included $110,000 ($971,359 adjusted) for motion picture rights and $25,000 ($220,763 adjusted) for theater television. There was no TV for local fans.[32]

Saddler collected $60,669 ($535,740 adjusted) of net for the fourth bout, Pep $36,401 ($321,440 adjusted).[33]

Fans numbering 38,781 attended the third fight grossing $262,118 ($2,497,125 adjusted). Pep received 45 percent of net and Saddler 15 percent.[34]

In the third fight, Pep collected $92,408 ($892,535 adjusted) and Saddler $30,802 ($297,505 adjusted).[35]

In their first fight Pep got 50 percent, Saddler 10 percent. In the second, Pep 30 percent and Saddler 30. It was reported that this was "... a concession that drew commendation for Saddler."[36]

---

*Sums adjusted for inflation using the CPI (Consumer Price Index) Inflation Calculator, U.S. Bureau of Labor Statistics, U.S. Department of Labor.

Fun fact: New ring floor for title fight

The old felt floor covering was replaced by a plastic composition known as ensolite. The material was used in planes, tanks and helmets. This followed a "precautionary campaign" instituted by the NYSAC that intensified with the death of Georgie Flores after a bout in Madison Square Garden. The new material was reported to have a higher safety value, but would not hamper performance.[37]

Aftermath

Busy day

On the same day Christenberry asked for the reports from officials, Saddler reported at the Army's pre-induction center for his physical examination and was ordered to report to Fort Jay for a further check, preliminary to being recalled for service. He served a brief period in the Navy during 1944.

Back in Hartford, a "disconsolate Willie Pep disclosed … he was thinking of retirement."[38]

Hammer comes down

The NYSAC held an open hearing regarding the fourth fight. At that hearing Christenberry told the two boxers, "You violated every rule in the book. It is the unanimous opinion that the punishment be affixed."[39] Saddler was suspended and Pep's license was revoked, the latter a much more serious punishment.

Charley Johnston, Saddler's manager, was penalized for interfering with Dr. Nardiello. He received a 33-day suspension and a fine of $100. Johnston said, "I shouldn't have done it. I'm sorry."[40] He was the only one apologizing that day.

Johnston took the opportunity to say that the suspension of his boxer was "a drastic decision against my boy."[41] He said that Pep was the real culprit and that "Saddler was never suspended and never questioned about his behavior in the ring."[42]

Both fighters were questioned. Christenberry said their actions had done much to "destroy the reputation of boxing and bring the game into disrepute."[43]

Pep said, "I didn't try to destroy the reputation of boxing. It is my livelihood and I want to continue boxing."[44]

Pep was asked why he did not listen to the referee's warnings. He said, "It seemed there was no referee in the fight. He was getting in too late to break us up. The only way I could get away from him (Saddler) was to wrestle him. He was holding me by the head and banging away at my eyes."[45]

Pep was sent out of the room and the commissioners conferred. He was called back and told that his license was revoked. He asked for how long. He was told, "You can always come back to the commission. The door is not closed."[46]

Then it was Saddler's turn. He said, "I thought I fought a clean fight."[47]

No dirty fighter says Pep
Regarding the holding and hitting complaint, Pep relaxed his view many years later.

In his book, *Friday's Heros*, Pep said, "Sandy was just rough and tough and not a 'dirty fighter' as people think. His almost five foot, ten inch frame [Saddler was 5' 8 1/2" — still quite tall for a feather], tremendous reach and the punching power of a welterweight, sometimes had the five foot, five inch opponent [referring to himself] tangling himself to get inside on Sandy."[48]

This view was shared by other boxing observers including A.J. Liebling in his book, *The Sweet Science*,[49] and (no surprise) Sandy Saddler.[50]

Christenberry asked, "You don't think the warnings of the referee were justified?"[51]

"No," said Saddler straightaway.[52]

Christenberry said, "Your opinion is contrary to the opinion of the judges and other observers at the ringside. And since you have no explanation for the tactics you employed, holding, hitting and continually violating virtually every rule in the book, and conduct detrimental to boxing, I hereby suspend your license indefinitely."[53]

The article goes on to say that Saddler will probably look to be reinstated in 30 to 60 days. But that "it is doubtful that Pep will get any consideration in the immediate future."[54]

Christenberry lifts suspension of Saddler
Saddler's ban was lifted 60 days later, and he was able to fight Paddy De Marco in Madison Square Garden on December 7, 1951.[55]

OK! I'm sorry already!

Pep's license was restored on March 27, 1953 — 17 months after being revoked. He apologized in person to the commission. He said, "I'm sorry over the way I acted. I won't lose my head again."[56]

It was his second application for reinstatement. The commission refused his first on March 27, 1952. At that time it was reported that he "expressed great resentment" and that he said "he was the victim of an injustice."[57]

Still at it!

In the same article it was reported that Saddler was disqualified on a foul in a fight with Armand Savoie, a Canadian lightweight, in Montreal on March 3, 1952. He was charged with "butting, heeling, elbowing and various other infractions." Since he was about to go into the Army, he was not suspended. But he was fined $500.

Fighting after the fourth fight

Saddler had 23 more fights until he was forced to quit due to an eye injury in 1957. He fought with 11 top 10 contenders and defended the featherweight title twice during that time.

He won 16, 14 by KO. Saddler lost 6 decisions and one bout on fouls.

After the last Pep fight, he spent two years in the Army, from September 1951 to January 1954. In that stretch he fought only four times.

Saddler retired undefeated as featherweight champ.

Pep fought 76(!) more fights, but had bouts with only three top-ranked fighters including one title fight. He lost all three.

Of those 76, fights he won 69, lost only 7 and scored 14 KOs. Pep retired for the first time in 1959 and made a comeback in 1965 at age 42. He fought 10 more times and lost just one of those fights, his last, on March 16, 1966.

Willie Pep vs. Sandy Saddler

Sources for Chapter 9

cyberboxingzone.com

Dickens, Charles. *Barnaby Rudge.*

Heller, Peter. *"In This Corner ...!": 42 World Champions Tell Their Stories.* New York, New York: Da Capo Press, 1994.

Liebling, A.J. *The Sweet Science.* New York, New York: North Point Press, 1956.

New York Times

Pep, Willie and Sacchi, Robert. *Friday's Heros.* Bloomington, Indiana: Author House, 2008.

Roberts, James B. and Skutt, Alexander G. *The Boxing Register.* Ithaca, New York: McBooks Press, Inc., 2011.

Footnotes for Chapter 9

1 *The New York Times*, March 1, 1951.
2 Ibid., June 3, 1951.
3 Ibid., August 28, 1951.
4 Ibid., December 4, 1951.
5 Charles Dickens, *Barnaby Rudge,* Chapter 29.
6 James B. Roberts and Alexander G. Skutt, *The Boxing Register* (Ithaca: McBooks Press, Inc., 2011), 677.
7 James P. Dawson, *The New York Times*, September 27,1951.
8 Ibid.
9 Ibid.
10 Ibid.
11 Mike Casey, *Slow train coming: Sandy Saddler and the long road to acceptance,* http://www.cyberboxingzone.com/boxing/casey/MC_Saddler.htm
12 Ibid.
13 James P. Dawson, *The New York Times*, September 27,1951.
14 Ibid.
15 Ibid.
16 Ibid.
17 Ibid.
18 Mike Casey, *Slow train coming: Sandy Saddler and the long road to acceptance,* http://www.cyberboxingzone.com/boxing/casey/MC_Saddler.htm
19 James P. Dawson, *The New York Times*, September 27,1951.
20 Ibid.
21 Ibid.
22 Willie Pep and Robert Sacchi, *Friday's Heros* (Bloomington: Author House), 17.
23 Mike Casey, *Slow train coming: Sandy Saddler and the long road to acceptance,* http://www.cyberboxingzone.com/boxing/casey/MC_Saddler.htm
24 Willie Pep and Robert Sacchi, *Friday's Heros* (Bloomington: Author House), 15.

25 James P. Dawson, *The New York Times*, September 27,1951.
26 Ibid.
27 Ibid.
28 Ibid.
29 Ibid.
30 Willie Pep and Robert Sacchi, *Friday's Heros* (Bloomington: Author House), 17.
31 *The New York Times*, September 19, 1951.
32 Ibid.
33 Ibid., September 28, 1951.
34 Ibid., September 10, 1950.
35 Ibid., September 23, 1951.
36 Ibid., January 5, 1949.
37 Ibid., September 22, 1951.
38 Ibid., September 28, 1951.
39 Ibid., October 6, 1951.
40 Ibid.
41 Ibid.
42 Ibid.
43 Ibid.
44 Ibid.
45 Ibid.
46 Ibid.
47 Ibid.
48 Willie Pep and Robert Sacchi, *Friday's Heros* (Bloomington: Author House), 19.
49 A.J. Liebling, *The Sweet Science* (New York: North Point Press), 207.
50 Peter Heller, *"In This Corner ...!": 42 World Champions Tell Their Stories* (New York: Da Capo Press), 292-293.
51 *The New York Times*, October 6, 1951.
52 Ibid.
53 Ibid.
54 Ibid.
55 Ibid., October 27,1951.
56 Ibid., March 28,1953.
57 Ibid., March 28,1952.

Willie Pep vs. Sandy Saddler

10. Fighting after Pep

It was Pep's victory over De Marco that instilled the overconfidence that led to Pep's demise in his first fight with Saddler.

It was reported that Saddler was interested in pursuing the lightweight crown and was confident that he could take out Jimmy Carter who held it at the time. Unfortunately his bid never got traction. That is, he got beat (in a nontitle fight) by the one guy who knew how to do so at exactly the wrong time. He lost two more fights after that and won once before induction. He entered the Army for a two-year hitch with his featherweight title on ice, his dreams of lightweight success in shambles and a bad boy reputation.

De Marco curse

Paddy De Marco presents an interesting case. He was good enough to be a champion, albeit for a very short time. De Marco won the lightweight crown March 5, 1954 by defeating Jimmy Carter. He lost it in the rematch the following November.

De Marco has a shared history with Pep and Saddler. Willy Pep decisioned De Marco September 10, 1948, about five months before he fought Saddler for a second time. Saddler fought De Marco three times, losing twice. It was Pep's victory over De Marco that instilled the overconfidence that led to Pep's demise in his first fight with Saddler.

It was this defeat from De Marco that derailed Saddler's campaign to gain the lightweight title.

Saddler fought De Marco for the third and final time on December 7, 1951, just a few weeks after defeating Pep for the last time. It was this defeat from De Marco that derailed Saddler's campaign to gain the lightweight title.

De Marco's "plunging, crouching style of fighting"[1] proved a puzzle to Saddler, and he lost on two of three cards. Saddler suffered swelling of the left eye and a cut over the left. De Marco was bruised about both eyes, but he kept "persevering on the attack."[2] Instead of reassessing the situation and the problem of the fiery fireplug, Saddler "became wild when he might have been effective."[3] There were rounds where the superior boxer and puncher showed himself, especially in the last two rounds, but apparently it was too little, too late for two of the judges. Saddler was very upset about the outcome and said New York was now "off limits"[4] regarding future fights. He in fact would not fight in New York again until January 15, 1954.

No answers
Five weeks later he met George Araujo in Boston and lost a unanimous decision. Again, Saddler had no answers. He was the aggressor, but landed no big punches. "Araujo was unmarked"[5] and Saddler "was worse for wear"[6] at fight's end with cuts on his forehead and left eye.

"You have no right"
Could things get worse?

On March 3, 1952 Sadder lost his nontitle fight with Armand Savoie in Montreal on fouls. Emile Gauthier, president of the Montreal Athletic Commission, climbed into the ring to stop the fight himself. Referee Tommy Sullivan said the official reason for the disqualification was "fouling continually — heeling, holding, hitting on the breaks and sending in low blows. It looked to me for a while as if he wanted to be disqualified."[7] At the weigh-in Gauthier, concerned about a foul-free bout, confronted Saddler and said he was known as a "dirty fighter."[8] Saddler got his back up and said, "you have no right to talk to me that way."[9]

Saddler seemed to have the upper hand with Savoie through three rounds despite numerous warnings from Referee Sullivan and having two of those rounds taken away. Before the start of the fourth, Gauthier told Sullivan to stop the fight. Later he even tried to freeze Saddler's purse, but was rebuffed by Matchmaker Raol Godbout who said, "I think you are exceeding your authority."[10]

Never one to back down, Saddler's manager Charlie Johnston was "incensed"[11] at the ruling and defended his fighters tactics to no avail. The confab in the ring was joined by an extremely disappointed crowd that "roared its disapproval."[12] Brawls broke out and three carloads of police were summoned to quell the uprising. Once again (like Havana), Saddler caused a near riot with his rough style of play, but this time without victory.

Coming back

In March 1952 Saddler enjoyed one of his finer ring moments when he TKO'd Tommy Collins in Boston in the fifth round. Saddler was all but KO'd in the first round — hammered and knocked down — and the next three rounds were hardly better.

In front on all the cards before the fifth, Collins pretty much had his way with Saddler and closed his left eye. But Saddler rallied with a combination of body and head shots with a splash of rough stuff (low blows, holding and hitting, forearm smash) and knocked Collins down three times before Referee Joe Zapustas "intervened."[13]

Coming back from the beating at the hands of the 23-year-old top contender cemented Saddler's claim to a fighter's heart. But the foul play was adding up. The "dirty fighter" rap was becoming of a piece with the tough guy reputation and it would eventually follow Saddler until the end of his days.

Coddled

Saddler did not fight again until January 1954. After Pep, he lost three of the four fights he had before entering the service — hardly an inspiring send off. He was still considered the featherweight champ, but the NBA decided to install an interim champion and conducted a tournament to establish one.

In *The New York Times* article dated March 22, 1952, it was reported that Saddler was inducted into the Army. It said he was "single and living with his parents at 749 St. Nicholas Avenue."[14] He said he wanted to continue boxing while in the service so he packed "boxing

Coming back from the beating at the hands of the 23-year-old top contender cemented Saddler's claim to a fighter's heart.

gloves, mouthpiece, head gear, sweat shirt and ring shoes."[15]

Apparently his time in the service was much better than Pep's. He coached and refereed boxing in Germany[16] and Fort Jay on Governors Island (located in New York Harbor) and eventually was promoted to corporal.

On March 16, 1954 he received a letter of commendation from Col. John S. Rossma, Deputy Post Commander at Fort Jay. The ceremony took place before a boxing match (Ward-Johnson) in New York City.[17]

The commendation, in part, states:

PFC Sandy Saddler (since promoted) is hereby commended for his efficient performance of duty as a soldier in the Army of the United States. His hard work, humility, and exemplary conduct were an inspiration to the troops with whom he has been associated.[18]

Was the service a hardship or unfair to Saddler? Far from it. A United States House of Representatives subcommittee heard arguments in July 1954 that certain professional athletes, Saddler in particular, were "coddled"[19] while in uniform. That there was a "glaring abuse of pass privileges."[20]

The second fight was memorable in that Charlie Slaughter up and quit in the fourth round muttering, "I was outclassed" as he left the ring.

The report, in part, said:

There was such a fortuitous concert of action and collaboration as to suggest loose conduct amounting to a fraud upon the Government which permitted this athlete to engage in a profitable contest, on Army pay and time, while coming from an overseas assignment on thirty days' leave, scheduling a fight to occur after his leave would have expired, posting a bond to perform, and then obtaining fifteen additional days' 'compassionate leave' because his wife had a cold.[21]

Of course, Charley Johnston had a rebutt. He said Saddler's wife was "suffering a more serious malady than a cold ... Mrs. Saddler and their young baby both were sick at the time."[22]

Saddler did in fact come back from his European assignment and get reassigned (most conveniently) to Fort Jay in New York. He was able to get passes to sign for and participate in three fights (with Bill Bossio, Charlie Slaughter and Augie Salazar) and, indeed, make some money. He did all this on "Army pay and time." But it was the Army that the government was mad at. Saddler served his time and, as previously stated, even received a commendation.[23]

After a 22-month layoff
In 1954 Saddler had nine fights, all nontitle, winning eight and knocking out seven including three top 10 contenders. He fought abroad in Caracas and Paris.

In the first of these fights, Joseph C. Nichols of *The New York Times* said, Saddler was "hardly the sharp-punching wizard who took the crown from Pep, but he didn't need much"[24] against Bill Bossio who stood a smidgen over five feet.

The second fight was memorable in that Charlie Slaughter up and quit in the fourth round muttering, "I was outclassed"[25] as he left the ring.

Against Augie Salazar it was reported that Saddler worked "in cool fashion"[26] and inflicted several cuts until Referee Tommy Rawson stopped it in the seventh. The article went on to say that Saddler "exhibited the rough and ready tactics for which he is known."[27]

In May Saddler suffered another one of those head-scratching defeats against the unranked Algerian, Hoacine Khalfi. The latter proved to be a "a speedy and elusive target"[28] and "refused to permit the New Yorker to get set." A "determined"[29] Saddler was the aggressor, but his attacks were successfully countered by Khalfi who must have had the fight of his life.

When would Saddler defend his title again?
In October 1954 the National Boxing Association (NBA) warned Saddler that he had to defend his title by December. He had not put the crown on the line since September 1951, when he TKO'd Pep in their fourth fight. Charlie Johnston was not impressed. He and Saddler were in Paris for a nontitle bout with European featherweight king Ray Famechon and said he was not worried about the NBA. In fact, they would stay and take fights in Europe "... if there's any money in it."[30]

On December 15, 1954 the NBA's recognition of Saddler ended. Tony Petronella, NBA president, said, "We don't have the power to strip Saddler of his title, but we are withdrawing recognition. The NBA is going to be very firm with champions on defending every six months."[31]

The NBA had a point. Champions need to fight. But who was gonna listen?

On cue, the ever defiant Johnston said Saddler would defend "when he's ready and that will be February."[32]

Robert K. Christenberry of the NYSAC said, "I have found the NBA hasn't always been a solid front. I also recall something about titles being won and lost in the ring."[33]

So much for the directives of the NBA.

French connection
Saddler's bout with Ray Famechon was notable because the Frenchman was not a tomato can — he was the European featherweight champ and had fought Pep for the world title back in March 1950. He lost a unanimous decision to Pep then and was TKO'd by Saddler on October 25, 1954.

Saddler "forced the fight all the way"[34] and, by the end of the fifth, Famechon's face was "a bloody pulp."[35] His corner wouldn't let him answer the bell for the sixth round "although he appeared strong and wrestled with them."[36]

Each weighed 128 1/2. This was Saddler's lowest weight since December 7, 1950 when he fought Del Flanagan.

Saddler "forced the fight all the way" and, by the end of the fifth, Famechon's face was "a bloody pulp."

1955

Saddler fought seven times in 1955 and won five bouts, four by KO or TKO. He faced three top 10 contenders and lost to two. He finally defended the featherweight title against Teddy "Red Top" Davis and won a unanimous decision. Following the money, Charlie Johnston took his fighters to Japan and Manila.

Lulu Perez

This January match was reported as "an effortless tune-up for Sandy's title match the next month against Teddy (Red Top) Davis."[38] Saddler "showed no more than a bead or two of perspiration"[39] after stopping Perez in the fourth round.

Besides owning a catchy first name, Perez is famous for another Pep connection — this one a bit deeper and darker than the rest. Perez TKO'd Pep in February 1954 in a fight many considered fixed. It was suggested many years later in a magazine article that Pep threw the fight which led to a court battle. More on this later when we step into Pep after his fighting days.

Red Top

Finally! A title fight.

The New York Times headline reads:

He didn't knock out all his opponents. It's just that he punched like King Kong and utilized the "almost illegal tactics" like a wizard — and those assets made for better copy.

Saddler Retains Title with Unanimous Decision over Davis

Champion Scores Easily at Garden

... Beats Davis with Skillful Fighting[40]

The ever articulate Joseph C. Nichols wrote:

Sandy turned in a fine exhibition. In so doing he earned the grudging praise of the onlookers, whom he alienated in the earlier session by his rough, almost illegal tactics.

In the earlier rounds, Saddler did everything but bite his foe, but in the closing sessions the champion was a model of ring behavior.[41]

Did you catch the biggest surprises in the heading? The most unusual statements in Nichol's report? Sure you did. They are "Skillful Fighting" and "model of ring behavior," respectively. Words not often associated with Sandy Saddler and describing the most noteworthy thing about this ho-hum title defense. The point is: Saddler knew how to box! He didn't knock out all his opponents. It's just that he punched like King Kong and utilized the "almost illegal tactics" like a wizard — and those assets made for better copy. Still do.

This match also served as subject for a famous (in boxing lit circles) essay by A.J. Liebling, *Great-and-a-Half Champion*. It was written for the *New Yorker* magazine and was reprinted in his book, *The Sweet Science*. From this article has come some of the most lasting descriptions of Saddler's physical presence and style. It serves and has served as a vital Saddler resource and has been a resource for this humble book.

This sentence, or parts thereof have appeared in most every Saddler bio:

He himself is built like a bundle of loosely joined fishing poles, but they are apparently pickled bamboo; he takes a good punch, and his thin arms and legs never seem to tire.[42]

One last point about this fight. Red Top's record before the fight stood at 108 fights with 48 defeats — more defeats "than any other challenger in a title fight in modern boxing history."[43] To be fair, it was reported that he was mismatched with heavier fighters early on and "became successful with those in his weight class."[44] Another sad case of poor — extremely poor — management.

At least he got a shot.

By the way, "Red Top" was the nickname given to Davis as a kid because he sported a red mop.

Saddler 124 1/2 pounds, Davis 126. It was reported that Saddler looked "overtrained."[45] That is, he looked skinnier than usual. But, obviously, his starved look masked a still lethal boxer.

Punched out by the wife
Only a few days before the Red Top scrap, Saddler's wife,

Helen, "filed suit for a legal separation on grounds of neglect, desertion and mental cruelty."[46] She was seeking $500 weekly alimony from his estimated $200,000 annual earnings and $10,000 for attorney fees. She charged that Saddler deserted her and their two small children, left her destitute and even refused to pay the $115 monthly rent on their apartment.

A settlement and a New York Supreme Court judgment regarding Saddler's obligation would be made in April 1960.[47]

Lopes upsets

Another bout where Saddler was off his game. Joey Lopes "scored a stunning ten-round decision"[48] over Saddler in Sacramento, California in May 1955.

Saddler held an "edge in the infighting."[49] But at range "Lopes scored repeatedly with long lefts and a sharp right hook."[50] Saddler took heavy blows in the second and ninth rounds and lost the fifth due to a foul.

Tokyo loves Sandy

In July 1955 Saddler TKO'd Shigeji Kaneko in six in Tokyo, but only after "Little Marciano"[51] gave it his all. Kaneko "carried the fight ... bullying and plastering the easy-going champion."[52] Saddler said his punches, "hurt me, shook me some."[53] But by the fifth the Japanese boxer was "near exhaustion."[54] Saddler dropped Kaneko in the sixth for an 8-count and Referee Jack Sullivan stopped it shortly thereafter.

Can't help noticing the phrase "easy-going" to describe Saddler. This is the only time I encountered such a

After all the troubles (a divorce, bad press, tough loss, NBA hassles) he was dealing with back home, he must have been thinking, God, it's great to be abroad!

description for a fighter usually painted in darker terms.

Perhaps an even more interesting aspect of this trip was the "rousing dignitary's welcome"[55] he received. *Jet Magazine* reported in it's July 28, 1955 issue that Saddler was put on parade "through the heart of Tokyo"[56] in a motorcade. An image shows the champion flanked by "two beautiful Japanese actresses."[57] Saddler waves and is all smiles. After all the troubles (a divorce, bad press, tough loss, NBA hassles) he was dealing with back home, he must have been thinking, *God, it's great to be abroad!*

It would take quite a while, but there would be a stateside parade for him and a slew of other boxing greats, including Jack Dempsey. That parade finally came about in October, 1968 — in New York, in Times Square, on Broadway.[58]

Manila does not
Sixteen days later, on the same Pacific Rim tour, Saddler lost a unanimous decision to Flash Elorde in Manila and nearly caused a riot. What rubbed the 10,000 "highly partisan"[59] fans the wrong way were Saddler's "infighting tactics"[60] that, no doubt, appeared like fouls. The Filipino judges thought so. They took rounds from Saddler because he "held, butted and hit with his elbows."[61]

Another rough fight, another near riot, another baffling defeat (baffling for those who thought, and think, Saddler is often the better fighter despite himself).

Charlie Johnston said, "This is the worst decision and the worst handling of a bout I've ever seen."[62] He said the police "did not give us any protection when the crowd got unruly."[63] A guy in Saddler's corner got hit with a flying bottle and received a three-inch gash. (Wild night!)

Although victorious, Elorde was judged by one Filipino judge to have "suffered a worse beating"[64] than Saddler.

Another rough fight, another near riot, another baffling defeat (baffling for those who thought, and think, Saddler is often the better fighter despite himself).

For better or worse, they are among the ways we remember Sandy Saddler.

1956 — End to an epic
In his last year of boxing, Saddler fought three times. He avenged his defeat with Elorde, defending his title for the last time in January; TKO'd Curley Monroe in February; and lost to top 10 contender Larry Boardman in April. In July he suffered eye and brain injuries from a car accident and never fought again. At the time he had been a world champion longer than any of the other current titleholders in boxing.

Saddler retired undefeated as featherweight champion

on January 12, 1957. Thus ending the Willie Pep and Sandy Saddler championship reigns that together lasted from November 1942 to January 1957 — 14 years of utter dominance and of some the greatest boxing (yet with a pinch of some of the worst) ever.

Flash falls

January saw Saddler successfully defending his title against Flash Elorde in San Francisco. It was raging and roughly fought. Elorde hammered Saddler in the sixth "with a barrage of lefts and rights to the jaw, with about six of his lefts landing."[65] Saddler opened a cut on Elorde's left eye in the seventh that would worsen in later rounds and undue him. But not before tearing into Saddler two rounds later causing his nose to "spurt blood."[66] Saddler suffered a cut over his right eye in the twelfth from an Elorde headbutt, a tactic that Saddler made even more use of. By the 13th round Referee Ray Flores and Dr. Robert Laddon agreed to stop the fight due to Elorde's eye.

An ugly, bloody win for Saddler with his signature blend of powerful punching and "rough"[67] methods. It was reported that "The champion continually massaged Elorde's face with his head whenever they were in the clinches. He spun Elorde, held him, hit him on the break a couple of times and in general had the pro-Elorde crowd booing all night."[68]

Saddler was ahead on all three cards at the stop.

The image that accompanied the article shows Saddler holding off Flash with a left as he makes futile effort to retrieve his mouthpiece from the canvas.

The last bout

Larry Boardman had Saddler on the ropes, literally and figuratively, early on. He was lucky to survive the first round.

Boardman scored with lefts, rights and uppercuts. Saddler landed only "one effective blow."[69] Although he was able to better fend off the assault by the sixth round, he never really established an offense of his own. The best thing the reporter could say about Saddler's performance "was his ability to take the pounding he received."[70] After punching Saddler around the ring, Boardman "settled down to outbox"[71] his man and to gain a unanimous decision over 10 rounds.

Saddler's infighting game was stifled by Boardman's "polished workmanship,"[72] and a vigilant Referee Joe Zapustas* who warned Saddler about hitting on the break and even took time out to give him a "short lecture."[73]

One of the most striking things in the report was that Saddler resorted to a "defensive fight"[74] in the middle rounds. Most unusual for this fighter — one of boxing's most aggressive warriors.

Was age a factor? Boardman was 20, Saddler 29. Willie Pep was 29 when he fought Saddler for the last time in 1951 and lost with a world record shiner.

Not this time
Remember Zapustas officiated the Saddler/Collins bout of March 1952 where Saddler's "rough stuff" was largely overlooked and contributed to his victory over Collins in the fifth round. Perhaps Referee Zapustas was less inclined to let Saddler fight his fight this time.

Sources for Chapter 10

Jet Magazine

The New York Times

Footnotes for Chapter 10

1 The New York Times, December 8, 1951.
2 Ibid.
3 Ibid.
4 Ibid
5 Ibid., January 15, 1952.
6 Ibid.
7 Ibid., March 4, 1952
8 Ibid.
9 Ibid.
10 Ibid.
11 Ibid.
12 Ibid.
13 Ibid., March 18, 1952.
14 Ibid., April 22, 1952.
15 Ibid.
16 Ibid., December 11, 1953.
17 Ibid., April 16, 1954.
18 Ibid.
19 Ibid., July 22, 1954.
20 Ibid.
21 Ibid.
22 Ibid.
23 Ibid.
24 Ibid., January 16, 1954.
25 Ibid., March 5, 1954.
26 Ibid., April 2, 1954.
27 Ibid.
28 Ibid., May 18, 1954.
29 Ibid.
30 Ibid., October 7, 1954.
31 Ibid., December 15, 1954.
32 Ibid.
33 Ibid.
34 Ibid., October 26, 1954.
35 Ibid.
36 Ibid.
37 Ibid., March 5, 1952.
38 Ibid., January 18, 1955.
39 Ibid.
40 Joseph C. Nichols, The New York Times, February 20, 1955.
41 Ibid.
42 Ibid.
43 Ibid.

"He himself is built like a bundle of loosely joined fishing poles, but they are apparently pickled bamboo; he takes a good punch, and his thin arms and legs never seem to tire."

— A.J. Liebling

44 Ibid.
45 Ibid.
46 *Jet Magazine*, April 3, 1955.
47 Ibid., April 7, 1960.
48 *The New York Times*, May 25, 1955
49 Ibid.
50 Ibid.
51 Ibid., July 9, 1955.
52 Ibid.
53 Ibid.
54 Ibid.
55 Jet, July 28, 1955.
56 Ibid.
57 Ibid.
58 *The New York Times*, October 17, 1968.
59 Ibid., July 21, 1955.
60 Ibid.
61 Ibid.
62 Ibid.
63 Ibid.
64 Ibid.
65 Ibid., January 19, 1956.
66 Ibid.
67 Ibid.
68 Ibid.
69 Ibid., April 15, 1956.
70 Ibid.
71 Ibid.
72 Ibid.
73 Ibid.
74 Ibid.

11. Fighting after Saddler

The way he lost deeply disappointed a certain type of boxing fan who believed in a fight to the finish.

Say die

Pep, of course, suffered from his Saddler defeats. He lost his invincibility. Twice champion of the world, he became a contender of debatable merit. The *way* he lost deeply disappointed a certain type of boxing fan who believed in a fight to the finish. Folks of this mindset think that fighters should never quit. They pay to see their professionals battle victoriously — or to suffer defeat with guns blazing. When Pep did not answer the bell in his third and fourth bouts with Saddler, he broke that code and (for these die hards) forever stained the Pep Legacy. Well, almost.

Because he is smarter and cleverer, the brunt of the blame has to be be borne by Willie the Wisp. There can be no acceptable excuse for his quitting in his corner. He's a professional being paid to go down, if necessary, but to go down with flags proudly flying. Abject surrender is a violation of the code and it shortchanges the customers.[1] Arthur Daley, *The New York Times.*

To be sure, the heavy weight of all those victories over three decades, coupled with the epic recovery from a plane crash have ensured a sacred place for Pep in the Boxing Universe. And I believe that the man's cheeky effervescence has played no small part in securing that place. We read about this fellow and can't help but think:

He continued to pile up the wins and often displayed the boxing acumen and physical talent that had taken him to the very top.

He was such a great guy on top of being such a great boxer!

His likability saw him through his defeats in and out of the ring.

Fighting on

After his last fight with Saddler, Pep remained on the scene for many years. He continued to pile up the wins and often displayed the boxing acumen and physical talent that had taken him to the very top. In clippings he is described as the "Old Master"[2] dispensing "boxing lessons."[3] He was an "elusive target"[4] with fast hands and feet who could make his opponent (usually called a "youngster"[5]) miss often and badly. But time takes its toll on every athlete. Losing a nanosecond here and there makes all the difference. And Pep relied on the nanosecond advantage as a boxer. He was not a powerful and dangerous puncher with an iron jaw. His success was built on speed, cleverness and stamina. As he grew older the blazing skills evaporated after the early rounds and he fell prey to younger, stronger fighters who could last. Whenever he was matched with a contender (after Saddler) — one of the true top-tier fighters — he lost. As a result, Pep never again fought in a championship bout.

Case in point: Tommy Collins drops his hero

On June 30, 1952 (nine months after the last Saddler

fight) Pep fought top 10 contender Tommy Collins* of Boston. It was reported that Collins "took a boxing lesson from Willie Pep for three rounds."[6] In those early sessions "Pep displayed much of his old-time skill"[7] and "pounded Collins' head and body with both hands and had the Boston youngster missing widely."[8]

Then Pep got caught.

Collins dropped Pep late in the fifth "with a terrific left flush to the jaw."[9] The bell saved him and he was carried back to his corner. Pep answered the bell for the sixth round, but was "unable to lift his arms as Collins belted him about the head with a merciless two-fisted attack."[10] Referee Joe Zapustas stopped it after fifty-five seconds.

This fight is noteworthy for the crashing defeat of a popular legend by another popular fighter and for a photograph taken at fight's end. In this image "published around the world,"[11] Collins is shown weeping after catching Pep with the left hook. When Pep went down Collins thought he had "severely hurt"[12] his hero.

*Collins is mostly remembered for a savage beating he took from lightweight champion Jimmy Carter in 1953. After being knocked down 10 times in the fourth round, his corner threw in the towel. The referee did nothing to stop the fight.

The carnage prompted federal investigation and resulted in the three-knockdown rule that is very common today — if a fighter is knocked down three times in a round the fight is stopped.[13]

To remind the reader, it was Collins who knocked down Saddler in March 1952 in a furious first round of fighting that almost did Saddler in. The latter finally came back in the fifth, knocking Collins down three times before the referee ended the bout.

Comeback trail

Pep fought and won 19 bouts until his next loss against Lulu Perez in February 1954. They included two TKOs and one KO. Articles are thick with Pep's intact boxing skills and his quest for another shot at the championship.

In his unanimous verdict over Texas lightweight champion Jackie Blair in May 1953, "Pep was too fast for the Dallas youngster."[14] The "ex-champion move[ed] along the comeback trail with an aggressive attack."[15]

Joseph C. Nichols of *The New York Times* wrote, "Willie Pep did an 'Old Master's' job on Pat Marcune of Coney Island"[16] on June 6, 1953. Pep "gave a splendid exhibition of boxing from the very first round, and he showed his rival tricks that Pat never could figure."[17]

Pep knocked out Marcune in the 10th after once again showing off superior boxing skills for nine rounds: "Moving in and out and from side to side, Willie threw everything at Pat from long range, while at close quarters he tied his foe up effectively."[18]

But not everybody bought into Pep's quest to regain stature. Arthur Daley of *The New York Times* wrote the day before the Marcune fight that Pep was "once one of the most remarkable fighters of this generation. He's just a journeyman performer now, just another hungry boxer looking for a payday."[19]

Daley went on to say that after the last Saddler fight the fans "never wanted to see Willie the Wonder again ... But time has healed the wounds and everyone feels sorry for

"... everyone feels sorry for Pep now, the fellow who once had fame, money and youth. He's lost them all."

Pep now, the fellow who once had fame, money and youth. He's lost them all."[20]

Then there was Lulu
Pep's fight with Lulu Perez on February 26, 1954 is a big problem for Pep fans. It was another losing battle with a top 10 contender after compiling a pretty good record after Collins. Pep's performance was lackluster resulting in a knockout and a forced "retirement"[21] from the New York Athletic Commission (Pep never fought in New York again). In fact, it was such a poor showing that it was assumed by many that Pep threw the fight.

Leading up to the Garden bout there was a modest buzz regarding Pep's chances — that he was "engaged in a last campaign spurred by the slim hope of earning one more chance at the crown."[22] He was still considered a boxing force "possessed of the great speed that carried him to the heights," but that he may not have the stamina to "go the distance"[23] with the "younger warrior."[24]

Film of the fight[25] survives and Pep's boxing is indeed ugly. Knocked down three times in the second round, Pep looks sluggish — showing nothing of the signature athleticism for which he was known and probably still capable of performing at the time of the bout. It appears that he is walking into punches. After three knockdowns the referee stopped the fight.

Pep gave it a good go. He "reached deep into his bagful of tricks and embarrassed Bassey on many occasions" — but he couldn't keep it up.

Perez shares some history with the aforementioned Tommy Collins, who was KO'd by Perez in December 1954. And Sandy Saddler? He KO'd Perez January 1955. The circle goes round.

The *New York Times* reported that Lou Viscusi, Pep's manager, met with the NYSAC in October 1954 and asked the commission to lift the suspension. He was told his fighter was not being suspended, but "retired" on the advice of the commission's medical board. Commissioner Christenberry said "We do not feel that Pep measures up to our standards physically."[26]

Losta wins, defeats when they matter
Pep fought 39 more times before his next fight with a top-ranked fighter. He lost only three and avenged one of those versus Gil Cadilli with a victory in a return match (the loss was a split decision and "booed by the crowd"[27]).

Reports regarding this stretch of activity against non-ranked fighters are much the same as before. In winning, Pep was described as having "too much experience"[28] for his younger foes and that he gave out "boxing lesson[s]"[29] to his baffled foes. One of his victims, Kid Campeche, said of his losing battle with Pep in March

1956: "Fighting Willie Pep is like putting out a grass fire."[30]

Kid Bassey

Kid Bassey was the last champion Pep fought. He met with the featherweight champ in a nontitle fight in Boston on January 26, 1959.

Pep gave it a good go. He "reached deep into his bagful of tricks and embarrassed Bassey on many occasions"[31] — but he couldn't keep it up. "Willie's ancient and much-traveled legs grew weary; he could not last the route."[32]

Although he came pretty close.

It was the same old story. After eight rounds, the 36-year-old ex-champ was leading on two cards. With just two rounds to go "Bassey's overhand rights ... solved Pep's tricky defenses."[33] Pep went down in the opening seconds of the ninth and went down again for the last time later in the same round.

"I saw my opportunity and I seized it," said Bassey. "I knew I had to do something with only two rounds left. However, I fought according to plan, especially going to the body to bring down Pep's guard."[34]

A "downcast"[35] Pep was asked if he would continue to fight. He said, "I don't see why not. This guy hits hard, and he hit me right. I made a mistake by pulling back instead of staying close, and that was it."[36]

The New York Times took a more sober view:

The outcome appeared to prove once again that youth, strength and punching power is too much for skill and experience alone. Bassey's victory crushed Pep's hopes for another title shot. No featherweight ever has won the championship three times.[37]

"The outcome appeared to prove once again that youth, strength and punching power is too much for skill and experience alone."

Pep fought his last top 10 fighter, Sonny Leon, on January 26, 1959 in Caracas (the only time he ever fought outside North America). He lost a ten-round decision (the only time he ever lost two in a row) and retired for the first time. He said a few days later, "I did a lot of thinking and decided it would be foolish to continue."[38]

But continue he did. In 1965 he made a comeback that lasted about 12 months. He fought 10 times and lost his last fight to Calvin Woodland on March 16, 1966.

He was 42 years old.

From July 1940 to March 1966 Pep amassed 229 wins, 11 loses and one draw.

The combined record for Pep and Saddler is 373-27-3.

Sources for Chapter 11

The New York Times

Prescott Evening Courier

Sugar, Bert Randolph. *Boxing's Greatest Fighters.* Guilford, Connecticut: The Lyons Press, 2006.

Footnotes for Chapter 11

1 Arthur Daley, *The New York Times*, September 28, 1951.
2 Joseph C. Nichols, *The New York Times*, June 6, 1953.
3 *The New York Times*, June 15, 1955.
4 Ibid., May 14, 1953.
5 Ibid.
6 *The New York Times*, July 1, 1952.
7 Ibid.
8 Ibid.
9 Ibid.
10 Ibid.
11 Gerald Eskenazi, *The New York Times*, June 6, 1996.
12 Ibid.
13 Ibid.
14 *The New York Times*, May 14, 1953.
15 Ibid.
16 Joseph C. Nichols, *The New York Times*, June 6, 1953.
17 Ibid.
18 Ibid.
19 Arthur Daley, *The New York Times,* June 4, 1953.
20 Ibid.
21 Ibid., October 23, 1954.
22 Ibid., February 26, 1954.
23 Ibid.
24 Ibid.
25 "Willie Pep vs. Lulu Perez," http://www.youtube.com/watch?v=Ylk465gqc6Q
26 *The New York Times*, October 23, 1954.
27 Ibid., May 19, 1955.
28 Ibid.
29 Ibid., June 15, 1955.
30 Bert Randolph Sugar, *Boxing's Greatest Fighters* (Gilford: The Lyons Press, 2006), 7.
31 *The New York Times*, September 21, 1958.
32 Ibid.
33 Ibid.
34 Ibid.
35 Ibid.
36 Ibid.
37 Ibid.
38 *Prescott Evening Courier*, January 29, 1959.

Willie Pep vs. Sandy Saddler

12. Saddler's final years

"I still don't believe any featherweight could whip me."

Hanging it up
A car accident injured both eyes on July 27, 1956, leaving Saddler "almost completely blind" in his right eye. It was reported that he suffered brain injury as well. Saddler held out hope and did not quit boxing right away, but didn't fight or defend his title as the NBA was clamoring for him to do.

In January, 1957 Saddler officially retired. Dr. Thomas W. Matthew, the director of neurosurgery at Coney Island Hospital in Brooklyn, said he recommended that Saddler give up fighting. He said, "There is no question that he will only aggravate the situation if he continues."[1] It was also reported that he had become "very nervous since the mishap as a result of the brain injury."[2]

Saddler, as terse and proud as ever, said, "Up to now I thought I could continue to box. I still don't believe any featherweight could whip me."[3]

A small article in *The New York Times* appeared the next month that said Saddler was seeing another specialist, Dr. Arthur Alexander Knapp, who claimed he could fix the damage. The retina of his right eye was detached and could be treated by "dehydration and diet."[4] Knapp's treatment was "successful in about a dozen cases."[5] On February 26 it was reported that the surgery was a "success"[6] and that a return to the ring was "possible."[7]

... Saddler could righteously say that he retired undefeated — an underappreciated fact for a somewhat underappreciated champion.

The treatment was, in fact, more than drying out and dieting. A "high-frequency electric current [was] used to cause an adhesion between the retina and the underlying tissue."[8]

But in the end the treatment did not work and Saddler never fought again. Elimination bouts were scheduled to fill the vacant featherweight title and Saddler could righteously say that he retired undefeated — an underappreciated fact for a somewhat underappreciated champion. This is what *The Ring: Boxing the 20th Century* has to say about Saddler's farewell:

"It was an ugly ending to an ugly, albeit dominant, reign."[9]

Some send off.

Coaching George Foreman
Saddler pursued a professional coaching career with some success while holding onto a day job as a trainer of amateur boxers for the National Maritime Union and the Police Athletic League in New York.[10] His most notable work was with a rising George Foreman in the early 1970s when Foreman trained for and fought Joe Frazier and Muhammad Ali in their legendary title bouts. He worked with a cousin, Dick Sadler (yes, only one "d" for this relative) and his old mentor, Archie Moore.

This, of course, must have been an extremely satisfying experience on a personal as well as a professional level. He was quoted in a number of articles around this time and enjoyed a taste of acclamation once again.[11]

Super slight

But before this high point there was a monumental slight that must have cut deeply. In 1963 Willie Pep was elected into The Ring Boxing Hall of Fame and Saddler was not. (This was the first Hall of Fame created by Nate Fleisher in 1954. In 1990 it would morph into the International Boxing Hall of Fame (IBHOF), located in Canastota, New York. This is the most recognized hall for boxing today.)[12]

Saddler was not inducted until 1971, eight years later. Perhaps with little wonder because it was *The Ring* magazine's Hall of Fame, the same institution that published *The Ring: Boxing in the 20th Century* that said Saddler's time as featherweight champ was so "ugly." But eight years in the wings behind the guy he defeated three out of four times? That's some ax to grind! A measure of justice arrived nearly 20 years later when the International Hall of Fame (IHOF) was created in 1990. At that time Pep and Saddler were inducted together with all the other deserving boxing greats.

"If you're black, get back"

Saddler was bitter about the lack of regard from the sporting world and never felt he got his just due after retirement. The ringing celebrations of Pep in the press and during various boxing ceremonies grated him to no end (especially during the years he waited to get into the Hall of Fame, no doubt). It didn't help that they usually showed up at the same function and usually got introduced together. In his interview with Peter Heller in the latter's book, *"In This Corner ..."* Saddler said,

"... Pep and I would be at a fight in the Garden, and they'll say, 'One of the greatest featherweights, Willie Pep. [And then they turn to me and say] here's another retired champ, Sandy Saddler' That's why I don't care to get introduced in the ring. Instead of saying, 'Sandy Saddler, the undefeated Featherweight Champion of the World,' instead [they say], 'Take it and like it. If you don't want it, leave it.' "[13]

He remained the unvarnished, straight talker until the end. That is, when he felt like saying something at all. To his way of thinking, the reason for the general rebuff was racism, plain and simple. Saddler said,

"[It's like they say], 'if you're white, you're right. If you're black, get back.' That's all there is to it. I'll lay my cards on the table. It's just plain old prejudice. The black man in this country, he have to do twice as hard as the white man to gain anything, and when he get it, for chrissake, they don't give him the recognition a man should get, and that's the whole thing in a nutshell. Just plain old prejudice. This country's built up on this sort of stuff."[14]

A lot of roughspeak here. And that crack about "This country's built up on this sort of stuff" back in the '70s probably did not win him a lot of friends in certain corners of the boxing community.

To be sure, Saddler's thorny and sullen demeanor ran counterpoint to the (mostly) peppy Pep, and one has to consider that personalities must have played some part in forming public feeling about these two. Pep was a likeable extrovert and Saddler was, well, maybe a little touchy.

Saddler faced and endured his detractors without the status that should have come with his remarkable career.

That is an injustice.

But Saddler was a black man in midcentury America and who are we to scoff at his torment. Jackie Robinson and Joe Louis were contemporaries and they had their burdens despite their heroic status. Saddler faced and endured his detractors without the status that should have come with his remarkable career.

That is an injustice.

"I'm not angry at Pep"

It should be noted that Saddler's animosity was never really directed at Pep. In the same interview with Heller, Saddler said, "I'm not angry at Pep at all. I'm angry at these other people who's pushing this thing. Pep and I are great friends."[15] Especially over time the sharper corners of their rivalry rounded, and they appeared together at various events.

There is a video of the two at an event where, as usual, they are paired at the podium. Pep has his patter down, telling jokes and having a great time with the audience. Saddler stands quietly with a grin in sunglasses and a baseball cap. Pep has his arm around his shoulders and encourages Saddler to say something, but it's apparent

"In the matter of skill and questionable tactics, Saddler and Pep probably hold the record."

that Saddler is struggling a bit to speak. Perhaps the dementia that would fall him (and later, Pep) was already clouding his mind. At any rate, Pep didn't skip a beat, fronted his former rival and somehow included him in the speech and celebration. They certainly looked like pals to me.

In 1968 Saddler was included in a Broadway motorcade in New York. The "Salute to Boxing" parade featured Jack Dempsey, Joe Frazier, Floyd Patterson, Sugar Ray Robinson, Rocky Graziano, Jose Torres, Jimmy Braddock, Carlos Ortiz, Ismaiel Laguna, Willie Pep, Joey Giardello, Tony Zale, Emile Griffith, Jake LaMotta and Nino Benvenuti.[16]

In 1973 he fought a for-fun exhibition with Pep at Madison Square Garden. It was reported that Pep was "a chubby 52" and Saddler "a slim 46."[17] Pep said, "I ain't mad at him, so I don't want him mad at me. When we fought, we used to bleed a lot but it was all my blood."[18] Saddler was "near fighting weight" and "looked almost as if he could step into a real main event."[19]

At the Garden exhibition were Jack Dempsey, Paul Berlenbach, Tony Galento, Jake LaMotta, Mickey Walker and Joey Giardello. Also present were Arthur Donavan, who refereed 20 heavyweight title fights, and Ruby Goldstein, who refereed 38 championship bouts. Both refs had their hands full with Pep and Saddler in days gone by.

An article about the event described the yin/yang or their rivalry concisely and accurately: "In the matter of skill and questionable tactics, Saddler and Pep probably hold the record."[20]

Although the furies had long since departed, personalities remained intact. The "irrepressible" Pep said, "If Sandy starts fighting in earnest, he's going to find himself in the ring alone." It was noted that Saddler "only grinned his reply."[21]

Bleak ending

It was reported that Saddler suffered in his final years. His demise is reminiscent of Henry Armstrong and Chalky Wright — champions who grew older without means. Saddler's case is heartbreaking. A proud man, alone, increasingly befuddled. Defenseless.

He was "swindled"[22] and lost what little money he had saved over the years. In 1989 he was beaten around the head with a heavy blunt object during a robbery.[23] The police found him wandering that night in Brooklyn, his wallet and his glasses lost. Saddler spent seven weeks in Bellevue Hospital Center where he was found to have dementia and memory loss.[24] He spent the last 10 years of his life in nursing homes.[25]

"I'm Sandy Saddler"

In his article[26] in the *New York Post* dated June 4, 2000, Jack Newfield described the mugging. At the time he was blind in one eye and suffering from Alzheimer's disease. He was "easy prey for the young thugs he would have put in the emergency room in his prime." They knocked off his glasses, cut off his pants, took his money and beat him. When the police found him all he could say was "I was featherweight champion of the world. I'm Sandy Saddler."

Finding a Ring 8 business card in his pocket, the cops called their number and Saddler was brought back from the "brink of homelessness." (Ring 8 was and still is a charitable organization that helps out those from the boxing community in need.)

Ring 8 fixed his teeth, got him new glasses and found him a place to live at the Kingsbridge Terrace nursing home in the Bronx (he had been living in a Harlem hovel without electricity). All of this was arranged by Ring 8 board chairman Charley Gellman. The latter chose the place partly because Phil Terranova, a rival to Saddler (and Pep) in their fighting days was living there.

Saddler was moved to the Schervier Nursing Care Center in the Bronx in 1994. He died September 18, 2001 of complications from Alzheimer's. He was 75.

Parting words

Saddler's son, Sandy Jr., had this to say to Tim Smith of the *New York Daily News*:

"He walked it like he talked it. He was a man of conviction who walked hard every day of his life. He didn't swear. He didn't drink and he didn't smoke. What he did, he brought everything to it."[27]

He went on to say, "Ray Arcel* told me once, 'Your father expects the same commitment that he expected from himself and there's only one Sandy Saddler. He was a hard man and he liked things done his way."[28]

About Ring 8

Taken from the Ring 8 website:
Formed in 1954 by an ex-prize-fighter, Jack Grebelsky, Ring 8 became the eighth subsidiary of what was then known as the National Veteran Boxers Association – hence, RING 8 – and today the organization's motto still remains: Boxers Helping Boxers.

RING 8 is fully committed to supporting less fortunate people in the boxing community who may require assistance in terms of paying rent, medical expenses, or whatever justifiable need.

www.ring8ny.com

Said Lou Duva** about Saddler and the current crop of fighters at the time, "Sandy would have taken them all apart."[29]

No doubt.

*Ray Arcel is among the most respected men in boxing history. He trained 20 world champions.

**Lou Duva was a boxer, manager, trainer, matchmaker and promoter. He worked the corner of champions Pernell Whitaker, Mark Breland, Evander Holyfield, Meldrick Taylor and Michael Moorer.

Source for these bios from *The Boxing Register.*[30]

Willie Pep vs. Sandy Saddler

Sources for Chapter 12

Heller, Peter. *"In This Corner ...!"*: *42 World Champions Tell Their Stories*. New York, New York: Da Capo Press, 1994.

New York Post

The New York Times

Pittsburgh Post-Gazette

Roberts, James B. and Skutt, Alexander G. *The Boxing Register*. Ithaca, New York: McBooks Press, Inc., 2011.

The Telegraph

Weston, Stanley and Farhood, Steven. *The Ring: Boxing The 20th Century*. New York: BDD Illustrated Books, 1993.

Footnotes for Chapter 12

1 *The New York Times*, January 23, 1957.
2 Ibid.
3 Ibid.
4 Ibid., February 7, 1957.
5 Ibid.
6 Ibid. February 26, 1957.
7 Ibid.
8 Ibid.
9 Stanley Weston and Steven Farhood, *The Ring: Boxing The 20th Century* (New York: BDD Illustrated Books, 1993), 118.
10 *The New York Times*, March 9, 1973.
11 Ibid., March 10, 1973.
12 Ibid., October 16, 1963.
13 Peter Heller, *"In This Corner ...!"*: *42 World Champions Tell Their Stories* (New York: Da Capo Press), 293.
14 Ibid.
15 Ibid.
16 *The New York Times*, October 17, 1968.
17 Ibid., March 7, 1973.
18 Ibid.
19 Ibid., March 10, 1973.
20 Ibid., March 9, 1973.
21 Ibid.
22 *Pittsburgh Post-Gazette*, September 21, 2001, from Tim Smith, "Sandy Saddler, Former Boxing Champion," *New York Daily News*.
23 *The Telegraph*, September 22, 2001.
24 Gerald Eskenazi, *The New York Times*, September 22, 2001.
25 *The Telegraph*, September 22, 2001.
26 Jack Newfield, *New York Post*, June 4, 2000.
27 *Pittsburgh Post-Gazette*, September 21, 2001, from Tim Smith, "Sandy

Saddler, Former Boxing Champion," *New York Daily News.*
28 Ibid.
29 Ibid.
30 James B. Roberts and Alexander G. Skutt, *The Boxing Register* (Ithaca: McBooks Press, Inc., 2011), 819.

Willie Pep vs. Sandy Saddler

13. Lulu and Newsweek

It wasn't so much a fix as "the sad, sad finish of an old fighter who, like hundreds before him, stayed around one fight too long."

Pep vs. Perez

On February 26, 1954 Pep fought Lulu Perez, a top 10 contender in New York City. The fight was a surprise on two counts. Pep, who was the number one contender and owner of a 23-1 record since his last Saddler fight in 1951, was knocked down three times in the second round bringing an automatic stop to the fight. The other surprise happened earlier, between the morning weigh-in and the opening bell, when "a flood of Perez money was wagered"[1] to change the odds from 6-5 Perez to 4-1. This kind of late wagering is called "smart money"[2] because those making such bets are thought to be privy to inside information — in this case, that Pep was throwing the fight.

There was something of an outcry at the time and "some New York papers had whispered"[3] fix, but there was nothing more solid to go on. Besides, it was pretty easy to say Pep was just getting old and rusty. After all, he was 32 and Perez was 20. Bill Lee of the *Hartford Courant* reported that Pep was a "hopeless wreck of a once great fighter."[4] It wasn't so much a fix as "the sad, sad finish of an old fighter who, like hundreds before him, stayed around one fight too long."[5]

Besides the sophomoric trick of not naming names, the magazine was certainly guilty of low bar journalism.

The way Pep lost is one thing and will no doubt fuel debate forever, but of greater importance at the time was the loss itself. The defeat knocked Pep out of contention. He would not fight another ranked fighter until 1959.

By the way, Saddler TKO'd Perez in January 1955 in a nontitle bout.

Fix?

And so things stood for many years ... until the summer of 1980. At the time *Newsweek* published a sports magazine call *Inside Sports*. In it's July issue there appeared an article titled "The Fix." The story was about a fighter (referenced only as "the Champ") who threw a fight for $16,000. Although actual names were not mentioned, all details regarding the fix and fight were "identical"[6] to those of the Pep vs. Perez battle. It was an expose without names — a curiously backhanded and (perhaps) cowardly way to hurl mud and sell magazines.

Three years after the article's publication, Pep filed a $75-million libel suit, claiming he loved boxing to much "to do such a thing"[7] as throw a fight.

Besides the sophomoric trick of not naming names, the magazine was certainly guilty of low bar journalism. The only source of the story, Norman Brett, was a compulsive gambler and an admitted pathological liar. Brett said his motive for the story was to ultimately make a book and a movie. Apparently he lost heart as this thing blew up. During the deposition Brett said he wished "this had never happened so I could go on with my life."[8]

Pep was fighting mad. About the story he said, "It's not so. I'm known all over the world. It lets me down. I don't care how messy it gets, I didn't do it."[9]

Pep's day in court

One can imagine what that courtroom scene looked like. On one side is Pep and his lawyer(s) and across the way the mighty *Newsweek* legal team, bristling with power and prestige. Keep in mind this was the early 80s, print media was king and *Newsweek* was a mighty force. It was Goliath against this little fellow, this former somebody working for the Connecticut State Athletic Department. And he did not own a magic slingshot.

Proving libel is not easy. Pep had to show that the magazine knew it was publishing false information and in the end he could not do that. It should be noted, however, that *Newsweek* wanted the court to issue a summary judgment in January 1983, a way to toss the case out before a jury can decide, and was denied. There was enough smell (lack of corroboration, unreliable source) to warrant the looksee of a federal jury.

Here's what the court had to say about dismissing the case outright:

It is true that a plaintiff in a libel suit against a public figure has a heavy burden of proof. He must show with "clear and convincing proof" that defendants published the libel with actual malice, that is, knowledge of falsity or reckless disregard for the truth.

Nevertheless, without making any finding on the merits, we conclude that on the record as it stands a reasonable jury could find with convincing clarity that Newsweek "in fact entertained serious doubts as to the truth of [the] publication."

Accordingly, the motion for summary judgment is denied.[10]

"When I got hit, I got hurt"

Described as "trim and 61,"[11] Pep had his day and say in court in February 1984. He denied he threw his bout against Lulu Perez. "I boxed all them fights and nobody hit me," he testified. "Finally when I got hit, I got hurt." He told the U.S. District Court in Manhattan that "Winning is my thing. Anything I do, I do to win."[12]

At the time he was the Connecticut state boxing inspector. It was reported that he said "he thought he might have been named state boxing commissioner were it not for the *Inside Sports* article."[13]

But after a two week trial, the end came with a terse "No," when the jury was asked if Pep had proved the story false. They had deliberated for 15 minutes.[14]

Results of verdict

Pep never got the commissioner's job, but there's no evidence that he was in line for it. Other than that, he won so many fights before (and after) it really doesn't put much of a dent in his reputation. The verdict had nothing to do with whether he went down for the Perez fight or not, anyway. He had to prove that *Newsweek* was putting out a story they knew to be false. A different animal and a very difficult thing to do.

Proving libel is not easy. Pep had to show that the magazine knew it was publishing false information and in the end he could not do that.

Looking at the film[15] of the fight in question one may come away thinking Pep lacked his legendary speed and movement. Or he had a bad night. Maybe both. But that he took a dive? Although some boxing observers think so, it's subjective.

Here's another way to look at this. Let's look at the scoreboard. *Inside Sports* eventually disappeared as did the print version of it's mothership, *Newsweek.*

Pep is among the greatest winners (and I couldn't find a bigger winner) in recorded boxing history. He will remain so many, many years from now, I'm sure.

With or without the accusations of a reprobate and a now defunct journal, one battle out of 241 is not such a big deal.

"Lulu hit me a couple of good punches"
What Pep said about his fight with Perez

The talk after this fight was that I didn't fight and that's bad publicity for any boxer. The facts were that Lulu was a good right hand puncher and he caught me cold. At the time I was thirty-two and had been in the ring for sixteen years. Lulu hit me a couple of good punches and when you're in your thirties you can't take the same punch you did in your twenties. Your body is older and punches hurt a lot more.

After the Lulu Perez bout, Dr. Vincent Nardiello, the chief medical officer the the New York State Athletic Commission, came into my dressing room to examine me. It was standard procedure to examine a boxer before and after each fight. Anyway, the doctor looks up my nose and says, "Kid, your reflexes are gone. It would be dangerous for you to fight again." I never thought my nose had anything to do with my reflexes; maybe they weren't what they used to be (my reflexes, that is) but they weren't gone, and certainly not up my nose. It didn't sound like medical advice but more like sour grapes for my poor showing against Perez. I had heard that he had a good bit of money on me.

The analysis by Nardiello not only hurt me personally but it put me out of New York* — the big fight town. I continued to box outside of New York State, any place that I could. I got some good purses and some bad, but the important thing was that I was boxing and winning. In fact, I won about sixty fights since the doctor looked up my nose in 1954 until my bout with featherweight champ Hogan "Kid" Bassey in 1958. That's more bouts than the average professional boxer has in his entire career, even when his reflexes were not gone.[16]

*Dr. Vincent Nardiello's post-fight examination compelled the NYSAC to "retire" Pep. He would never fight in New York again. This was a very big deal back in 1954 since New York was the epicenter of boxing. Pep would continue to fight elsewhere, but nevermore under the bright lights of the Big Apple.

Source for this article from Willie Pep's book, *Friday's Heros.*

Sources for Chapter 13

Hartford Courant

Pep, Willie and Sacchi, Robert. *Friday's Heros*. Bloomington, Indiana: Author House, 2008.

The Tuscaloosa News

Weston, Stanley and Farhood, Steven. *The Ring: Boxing The 20th Century*. New York: BDD Illustrated Books, 1993.

Footnotes for Chapter 13

1 Stanley Weston and Steven Farhood, *The Ring: Boxing The 20th Century* (New York: BDD Illustrated Books, 1993), 106.
2 Ibid.
3 Terry Price, *Hartford Courant*, November 24, 2006.
4 Ibid.
5 Ibid.
6 Stanley Weston and Steven Farhood, *The Ring: Boxing The 20th Century* (New York: BDD Illustrated Books, 1993), 106.
7 Ibid.
8 Terry Price, *Hartford Courant*, November 24, 2006.
9 Ibid.
10 PEP v. NEWSWEEK, INC., 553 F. Supp. 1000 (S.D.N.Y. 01/5/1983).
11 *The Tuscaloosa News*, February 22, 1984.
12 Ibid.
13 Ibid.
14 Terry Price, *Hartford Courant*, November 24, 2006.
15 "Willie Pep vs. Lulu Perez," http://www.youtube.com/watch?v=Ylk465gqc6Q
16 Willie Pep and Robert Sacchi, *Friday's Heros* (Bloomington: Author House). 77.

Willie Pep vs. Sandy Saddler

14. Pep's long after

Pep worked 26 bouts as a referee from 1947 to 1971 — 23 of those between 1959 and 1971. These included five title fights.

Life outside the ring

After the fight game, Pep kept himself busy with work, friends and family. He worked as a state official in boxing and law enforcement; kept up with friends and associates in boxing circles; and became a celebrated and cherished citizen of the Hartford community. Although his family life was punctuated with marriage woes, he apparently did not spend a great deal of time alone. Even toward the end, Pep had people around him who cared — unlike Saddler, it seems, who kept to himself as he diminished and fell into the cracks.

At various times, Pep was a referee, a Connecticut state tax marshal, a Connecticut state boxing official and a special deputy for the Hartford Sheriff's Department.[1] He made numerous personal appearances and wrote a book, *Willie Pep Remembers ... Friday's Heros* that was published in the early 1970s (and has served as a resource for this book).

Pep as ref

Pep worked 26 bouts as a referee from 1947 to 1971 — 23 of those between 1959 and 1971. These included five

Governor Thomas Meskill said it was "Pep's association with questionable characters that was the problem."

title fights.[2]

Pep, however, worked only one Connecticut fight (in 1959).[3] In 1973 he was refused a license in that state by the boxing commissioner because of a damning state police report. Although the report was not made public, Governor Thomas Meskill said it was "Pep's association with questionable characters that was the problem."[4]

Perhaps Meskill was suggesting Pep knew folks who lived in the margins and had ties to gambling and criminal activity. This was a whispered topic in many conversations about Pep. In his book, *Jacobs Beach*, Kevin Mitchell calls Pep "darling of the Mob,"[5] but doesn't provide a whole lot of detail. Of course, there was the alleged fix of his fight with Lulu Perez which supposedly was tied to gambling debt. One can easily imagine Pep talking to some bad guys, sure. There were lots of mob guys around in those days. But Pep liked to talk to everybody. In the end, there is enough dirt to tantalize, but not to indict.

Pep fought to make the report public to no avail. He said, "It's not my license that is at stake, it is my reputation. I have never dishonored my profession, nor my title, and I have tried to do as many charitable things as I could for this state."[6]

As things worked out, perhaps his "association" wasn't that compelling. Pep was hired by the state as a deputy boxing inspector soon after the fuss, a position he held for several years.[7]

Bad night down under

Pep holds a respectable record as a referee, but he suffered one bad outing. On July 28, 1969 at Sydney Stadium, Pep refereed a WBC featherweight title fight between Johnny Famechon and Fighting Harada.

There were errors made. In the fifth round, Harada slipped, but Pep ruled it a knockdown. In the 11th, Famechon was knocked down, but Pep ruled it a slip. Pep was the sole judge and ruled the bout a draw. But after officials checked Pep's card, they noticed he had added the final tally incorrectly. Famechon was ahead by one point.

Even though Famechon was the local favorite, the crowd voiced it's disapproval. It was deemed "a horrible decision; even the local newspapers gave it to Harada."[8] This was the last championship match Pep would referee.

Pep as Connecticut boxing official

Pep served his home state of Connecticut and boxing as a "member of the State Athletic Division, which supervises boxing and wrestling in the state under the Consumer Protection Department."

He was referred to as a "commission member" and/or an "inspector" in various articles describing official state boxing business, issues and functions. Issues that Pep helped review included prison boxing (in Connecticut)[9]

Pep's one-liners

There are three things that go on a fighter, first your reflexes, then your chin, then your friends.

I've got it made. I've got a wife and a TV set and they're both working.

They call Ray Robinson the best fighter, pound for pound. I'm the best fighter, ounce for ounce.

An old opponent walked up to me and asked, "Do you recognize me?" I looked hard and considered before saying, "Lie down so I can recognize you."

I'm all right until I hear a bell.

Who was the best person I ever fought? My third ex-wife.

My fight style is "He who hits and runs away lives to fight another day." And that's what I did for 29 years. I tried to hit and get away. And I did. I got away with it.

He woulda been champion if it wasn't for his bad hands — referee kept stepping on 'em.

Went to the doctor for a physical before I got married last time. "Aren't you worried about marrying a younger woman?" he asked. I told him, "Doc, if she dies, she dies."

From a variety of sources including Jim Shea, *Sports Illustrated*, July 16, 1990.

Keven Rooney, shouted, "Willie Pep[!] Willie Pep[!] in order to get his boy Vinny to box more effectively. And it worked. Vinny won in 12.

and boxing safety. The latter drew the attention of seven other state commissions who met after the ring death of Duk Koo Kim in November, 1982.[10]

Pep's ambition was to be the Connecticut State Boxing Commissioner, but those plans were thwarted (according to Pep) because of the 1980 article in *Inside Sports* magazine about that fight he was more or less accused of throwing[11] (see previous chapter).

Always a hit

Pep was a regular at boxing functions. It was said that "whenever a boxing affair need[ed] dressing up, Pep [got] a call" and was "always a hit at boxing dinners."[12] He had an "arsenal of one-liners and a Dangerfieldesque delivery"[13] that kept them in stitches (a few are listed stage left.)

Respected

Pep's reputation as a boxer's boxer was burnished over time and celebrated by a who's who of modern fighters, trainers and the boxing press.

Ray Mancini, a WBA lightweight champ, was shadow-boxing in front of reporters while training for a title fight in 1989 and said out loud, "Just like Willie Pep, huh?

De La Hoya "desperately wanted to impress [Pep]" and had Pep's legendary punchless round in mind ...

Who says I can't box?"[14] Maybe he was just joking. Consensus was that he could not or would not box. Mancini was known for his bloody brawling.

In 1993 Buddy McGirt, a WBC welterweight champion, was happy to learn a few of the old tricks from the old man:

"Willie Pep told me, 'Let me show you the spin move that won most of my fights for me,'" McGirt recalled, leaning into a crouch. "He said, 'I grab your right arm with my left hand, then I grab your left arm with my right hand, spin you to the left and stay behind you.' He told me that's how he got out of danger."[15]

Six months later, in *The New York Times* article about Pernell Whitaker, a winner of world titles in four weight classes, writer Gerald Eskenazi said, "Whitaker's spiritual boxing ancestor is the wily Willie Pep of five decades ago ..."[16]

Super middleweight champ Vinny Pazienza was busy with Roberto Duran during one of his title fights in 1995 when his trainer, Keven Rooney, shouted, "Willie Pep[!] Willie Pep[!]"[17] in order to get his boy Vinny to box more effectively. And it worked. Vinny won in 12.

In 1996, Eskenazi again brought up Pep in a column about Roy Jones Jr. He wrote, "If Roy Jones Jr. is not the world's greatest fighter already, then someone else out there is giving a pretty good imitation of Sugar Ray Robinson or Willie Pep or Muhammad Ali. And actually, no one is, except Jones."[18]

Pep and De La Hoya

Oscar De La Hoya (a champion many times over) was particularly enthusiastic about Pep.

For a fight with Caesar Chavez in 1996, it was reported in *The New York Times* that De La Hoya became a student of all things Pep. "His training included replaying tapes of Willie Pep, the great old featherweight champion and a boxer of unsurpassed skills."[19]

De La Hoya took the next step about six months later by flying a 73-year-old Pep out for his title bout with Miguel Angel Gonzalez. "De La Hoya's entourage tonight included a new face — Willie Pep. Two years ago, De La Hoya did not know Willie Pep from Willie Mays, but his new trainer, Jesus (the Professor) Rivero, had dusted off some of Pep's old fight films to show his pupil what real footwork was."

The article went on to say that Pep "was clearly impressed by De La Hoya's stone hands, but stopped short of calling him the best he had ever seen."[20]

In a follow up column by Tom Friend a day later, it was reported that De La Hoya "desperately wanted to impress [Pep]" and had Pep's legendary punchless round in mind. "But De La Hoya's attempt at a no-hitter failed.

He did not throw a punch in the last half of that third round — choosing instead to shadowbox — and it was the only round he lost until the ninth. 'Well, I felt pressure with Willie Pep actually being there,' De La Hoya said."[21]

For his fight with David Kamau in June, 1997, De La Hoya's trainer, Emanuel Steward, had had enough of the Pep influence. For the hard-punching Kamau he asked De La Hoya to get back to power boxing and "tried to break him of the bob-and-counter style of the fighter's hero, Willie Pep."[22] Steward said of De La Hoya, "He's 5 foot 11 — it doesn't make sense to have him balled up."[23]

Pep and Pacquiao
In 2009, Richard Sandomir of *The New York Times* wrote that Mannie Pacquiao was "infusing fresh life"[24] into boxing and compared his influence with that of Sugar Ray Robinson, Willie Pep and Ray Leonard.

Pep gambling, investments, marriages
Pep was not particularly good with money or marriage. He gambled and lost, made poor business investments and married six(!) times. When asked about his decision to come back in 1965 he said, "I needed the money. Where else could I make $50,000 a year? I didn't have a trade ..."[25]

Pep made as much as $90,000 for a bout, but didn't have a lot to show for it. He always joked that he made $1.3 million in boxing and lost $1.4 million.[26]

Pep's fondness for gambling and the horses was well known. As he used to say, his financial downfall was "fast

As he used to say, his financial down- fall was "fast women and slow horses."

women and slow horses."[27] (It was reported that he was arrested in a dice game and fined $15 in 1946. Just the one time — maybe he was just careful about craps.)

His first four wives included a hometown sweetheart, a model, an exotic dancer and a hatcheck girl. "I never went looking for women," says Pep. "They were always around because I was in the limelight."[28]

Fortunately, his last two marriages had some longevity, especially his last. He married his sixth wife, Barbara, in 1987 and that lasted until his death on Thanksgiving day, 2006. By that time his family included four children, three stepchildren, four grandchildren, two great grand-children and several nieces and nephews.[29]

After retiring from his last job with the Sheriff's Department, he lived on a state pension and Social Security.[30] It was reported that Pep lived "modestly." He drove a Ford Escort and lived in his old neighborhood, just across the Hartford-Wethersfield border in Connecticut.[31]

Privately, Pep had a tight circle of friends who looked out for him. He was generally genial and renowned as a joke teller.[32]

Like it did Saddler, dementia took its toll in later years.

"And hey, I was champion of the world, and that still has its good days."

He spent the last six years of his life in an Alzheimer's disease unit at the Haven Health Center in Rocky Hill, Connecticut. Pep died at 84 on November 23, 2006.[33]

Unlike Sandy Saddler, Pep had something of a send off. Among those attending the wake were two Superior Court Judges and a former state legislator. Attending the funeral was the Director of the Department of Public Safety — which oversaw amateur and professional boxing in Connecticut at the time.[34]

Pep summing up

"I'd fight the same way. I wouldn't change my style. But, hey, maybe there are better fighters now, I don't know. The money would be great. Cripes, a .200 hitter in baseball makes a million a year. I made $1.3 million in my career, and my purses were cut 50 percent. One thing I'd do is get a financial adviser. Of course, who knows if I'd listen to him. But I got no regrets.

"And hey, I was champion of the world, and that still has its good days."[35]

"I'm crazy over boxing, always have been, always will be. I think it's the fairest of all sports, man against man, no two-one or three-one situations as develop in, say, football or basketball. And it's best to watch when done reasonably well. In other words, when two men stand up there and fight with their brains as well as their brawn."[36]

He carried boxing beyond the coarse, vulgar displays of human carnage. His were classic victories, rarely bloody; more the incredibly skilled surgeon, operating on his foe with the cool dispassionate dispatch of the antiseptic clinic ... He is the greatest athlete in his particular specialty I have ever seen.

Don Riley

Don Riley was a writer for the *Pioneer Press* and a broadcaster. He is best known in boxing circles for his role in the infamous Willie Pep-Jackie Graves "Round Without a Punch" controversy.

Willie Pep vs. Sandy Saddler

Sources for Chapter 14

boxrec.com

Harford Courant

Mitchell, Kevin. *Jacobs Beach*. New York: Pegasus Books, 2010.

The New York Times

Sports Illustrated

thesweetscience.com

The Tuscaloosa News

Weston, Stanley and Farhood, Steven. *The Ring: Boxing The 20th Century*. New York: BDD Illustrated Books, 1993.

Footnotes for Chapter 14

1 Matt Eagan, *Harford Courant*, December 31, 1999.
2 boxrec.com,
   http://boxrec.com/list_bouts.php?human_id=000043&cat=referee
3 Ibid.
4 Terry Price, *Hartford Courant*, November 24, 2006.
5 Kevin Mitchell, *Jacobs Beach* (New York: Pegasus Books, 2010), 238.
6 Terry Price, *Hartford Courant*, November 24, 2006.
7 Ibid.
8 Stanley Weston and Steven Farhood, *The Ring: Boxing The 20th Century* (New York: BDD Illustrated Books, 1993), 189.
9 *The New York Times*, February 10, 1980.
10 Ibid., January 21, 1983.
11 *The Tuscaloosa News*, February 22, 1984.
12 Jim Shea, *Sports Illustrated*, July 16, 1990.
13 Terry Price, *Hartford Courant*, November 24, 2006.
14 *The New York Times*, March 6, 1989.
15 Ibid., March 1, 1993.
16 Ibid., September 1, 1993.
17 Ibid., January 16, 1995.
18 Ibid., January 8, 1996.
19 Ibid., June 7, 1996.
20 Ibid., January 19,1997.
21 Ibid., January 20, 1997.
22 Ibid., June 12, 1997.
23 Ibid.
24 Ibid., December 30, 2009.
25 Jim Shea, *Sports Illustrated*, July 16, 1990.
26 Terry Price, *Hartford Courant*, November 24, 2006.
27 Ibid.
28 Jim Shea, *Sports Illustrated*, July 16, 1990.

29 Hartford Courant, November 25, 2006.
30 Jim Shea, *Sports Illustrated*, July 16, 1990.
31 Matt Eagan, Harford Courant, December 31, 1999.
32 Terry Price, *Hartford Courant*, November 24, 2006.
33 Richard Goldstein, *The New York Times*, November 25, 2006.
34 Tom Puleo, *Hartford Courant*, November 29. 2006.
35 Jim Shea, *Sports Illustrated*, July 16, 1990.
36 thesweetscience.com, www.thesweetscience.com/columnists/joe-rein/4684-few-did-it-as-well-as-willie-pep (Probably from *Boxing's Unforgettable Fights* by Lester Bromberg, Ronald Press, 1962.)

Willie Pep vs. Sandy Saddler

Acknowledgments

There are numerous sources for this book and are listed at the end of each chapter. Here are the ones that were especially valuable to this project.

The New York Times
These archives are pure gold and provided the guts of my research. The king of midcentury media was print, and the epicenter of boxing was New York City. It makes perfect sense that the best way to know what happened at the fights then is to read about them in *The New York Times*. The giants of ringside writing were Joseph C. Nichols and James P. Dawson. Their reporting and prose are incomparable

The Arc of Boxing:
The Rise and Decline of the Sweet Science
Mike Silvers' take on boxing history is especially good. His ideas regarding old school and new school boxing are well thought out, backed by research and inter-views with boxing insiders. Probably one of the best overviews there is. It contains tons of wonderful images.

"In This Corner ...!"
Forty World Champions Tell Their Stories
Peter Heller tracked down 40 great fighters, turned on the recorder and let them talk. His effort is an invalu-able resource and a great service to the sport of boxing.

The Boxing Register:
International Boxing Hall of Fame
Official Record Book
The ultimate boxing source. History, biographies, photos galore and, of course, stats. This title is indispensable.

Willie Pep Remembers ... Fridays Heros
(with Robert Sacchi)
This book was the first thing I read when I began looking into the project. It's pure Pep. It's all over the place, but it works. His humor and heart jump off the pages.

The Ring: Boxing The 20th Century
A terrific history with spot-on reporting and lively commentary. Broken down by decade and individual years with loads and loads of pictures.

My heros
My forte has always been instructional guides. At this time I have published six boxing books, and they have sold pretty well over the years.

I was inspired to try to write this kind of book, a history and biography, by a number of writers who do this so well. Great ones include Doris Kearns Goodwin, Evan Thomas, James McPherson and Edmund Morris.

They are the stars I look up to.

Index

Willie Pep vs. Sandy Saddler

Doug Werner is the author and/or publisher of several boxing guides including *Boxer's Start-Up, Fighting Fit, Boxing's Ten Commandments, Boxing Mastery, Boxer's Book of Conditioning & Drilling* and *Boxer's Bible of Counterpunching.* He is also the author of eleven books in the Start-Up Sports series®. He lives in Chula Vista, California.